Bali is the original magical isle. From the earliest years after its bloody incorporation into the expanding territories of the Dutch East Indies in the early 20th century, Westerners have been entranced by the heady combination of fabulous landscape and mesmerizing culture. Streams cascade down impossibly green mountainsides from sacred crater lakes, while dance dramas are performed to please the gods. Artists and the artistically inclined settled, worked and died amidst the rice fields and temples, reluctant to leave their Garden of Eden.

The advent of cheap air travel has brought increasing numbers of visitors, interested more in the attractions of the beach than of the temple and theatre. Today, hundreds of thousands of people visit Bali, many scarcely aware of the world beyond the sun lounger and the cocktail shaker. But while Bali may have changed – and the notion that the island is on the verge of being 'ruined' is a constant motif in writings about the island from the 1930s – the singular magic of the place has not been erased.

Lombok has been earmarked for tourist development for decades, on the pretext that it is in a position to emulate Bali's success. Whether the development plans will ever come to fruition is another matter and for the time being it remains a relatively quiet alternative to Bali, although considerably busier and more developed than the islands to the east. The number of visitors to Lombok is generally dependent on the numbers visiting Bali, and since the bombs, tourism in Lombok has very much taken a beating. While there are a number of first-class hotels along the beaches away from these tourist areas, Lombok is still 'traditional' and foreigners are a comparative novelty.

Planning your trip

Getting to Bali

Denpasar's airport, **Ngurah Rai**, is very well connected with the rest of Indonesia with frequent flights throughout the country. The many flights to Mataram (Lombok) cost around US$45 and take only 30 minutes. Budget carriers flying into Bali include **Jetstar Asia** (www.jetstarasia.com) from Singapore, and **AirAsia** (www.airasia.com), which flies direct from Singapore, Bangkok, Kuala Lumpur and Darwin. For more airport details, see page 22.

Getting to Lombok

Carriers flying to Lombok include **SilkAir** (T0370 633987, www.silkair.com), flying from Singapore four times weekly, and **Merpati** (T0370 621111), flying from Kuala Lumpur, Malaysia. **Garuda** and **Malaysian Airlines** also codeshare a route from Kuala Lumpur, via Jakarta. Internal carriers linking the Indonesian islands include **Lion Air** (T0370 663444, www.lionair.co.id), **Garuda** (T0370 646846, www.garuda-indonesia.com), **Merpati** and **Batavia Air** (T0370 648998, www.batavia-air.co.id).

Airport information **Selaparang Mataram Airport** lies north of Mataram and 20 minutes south of Senggigi Beach. It is possible to pick up a VOA (visa on arrival) at the airport. There is a money changer, information office and hotel booking counters. There are fixed-fare taxis from the airport to various destinations, bemos from the main road and a public bus to Bangsal (public bus towards Tanjung, ask to be dropped off at Pemenang. They are 500 m from the airport, to the left. When you reach the first crossroads, turn left and wait for your bus connection). International departure tax is 100,000Rp. Domestic tax is 30,000Rp.

   Note This airport is due to be replaced by Lombok International Airport located in the town of Praya to the south of Mataram in late 2011.

Getting around Bali

The main form of the local transport is the bemo (a small van). Travel by bemo often requires several changes, especially in the south, and most trips are routed through Denpasar, where there are five different bemo terminals in different parts of town, serving different directions. It can be almost as cheap and a lot quicker to charter a bemo or catch the tourist shuttle bus. In recent years bemo services have been significantly pared back and with the fairly efficient and cheap tourist shuttle bus service, foreigners are a rare sight on a bemo. It is also worth noting that bemo services are less frequent in the afternoons, and away from tourist centres are almost non-existent after night-fall. **Note** Taxi/bemo drivers can be very pushy and find it hard to believe you may be happy to walk. Expect to be asked for double the correct fare. Always use registered bemos, which have yellow-and-black licence plates. For a list of the key bemo terminals around Denpasar, see Transport, page 24.

Getting around Lombok

Lombok's main artery is the excellent road running east from Mataram to Labuhan Lombok and good paved roads to Lembar, Praya, Kuta and to Bangsal in the north. Most of Lombok's roads are paved, but the secondary roads are not well maintained and car travel can be slow and uncomfortable, plus there are hazards of potholes and random rocks.

Bemos and colts are the main forms of transport and a good cheap way to get around the island and, unlike Bali, frequent changes of bemo are not necessary to get from A to B.

Perama ① *Jln Pejanggik 66, Mataram, T0370 635928*, operates shuttle buses from Bali to Lombok, offers tours and transport within Lombok, and provides onwards transport to Flores via Komodo.

Cidomos are a two-wheeled horse-drawn cart. In the west, cidomos are steadily being replaced by motorbikes and bemos, but in the less developed central and east they remain the main mode of local transport and are more elaborate, with brightly coloured carts and ponies decked out with pompoms and bells.

Sleeping → *For hotel price codes, see box on next page.*

Tourist and business centres usually have a good range of accommodation for all budgets. Bali, for example, has some of the finest hotels in the world – at a corresponding price – along with excellent mid- and lower-range accommodation. However, visitors venturing off the beaten track may find hotels restricted to dingy and over-priced establishments catering for local businessmen and officials. The best-run and most competitively priced budget accommodation is found in popular tourist spots – like Bali and Yogya. It is almost always worth bargaining. This is particularly true for hotels in tourist destinations that attract a fair amount of local weekend business: the weekday room rate may be 50% less than the weekend rate. All hotels are required to display their room rates (for every category of room) on a *daftar harga*, or price list. This is invariably either in public view in the reception area or will be produced when you ask about room rates. Indonesians prefer to be on the ground floor, so rooms on higher floors are usually cheaper. In cheaper accommodation, the bed may consist only of a bottom sheet and pillow with no top sheet.

Terminology can be confusing: a *losmen* is a lower price range hotel (in parts of Sumatra and in some other areas, *losmen* are known as *penginapan*); a *wisma* is a guesthouse, but these can range in price from cheap to moderately expensive; finally, a *hotel* is a hotel, but can range from the cheap and squalid up to a Hilton.

With the economy faring well in Indonesia in recent years, and a more affluent middle class emerging, mid-range and top-end hotels are being built at an extraordinary rate, many offering excellent promotion rates and possessing all the mod cons an international traveller requires. The backpacker market has seen less money being poured into it than, for example, in Malaysia and Thailand, and these places can often seem to be a bit bleak and tawdry compared to cheaper digs elsewhere in Southeast Asia. The exception to this is in Bali and some parts of Lombok, where the backpacker market is still pulling in the rupiah and there are a few gems to be found.

Bathing and toilets

Baths and showers are not a feature of many cheaper *losmen*. Instead a *mandi* (a water tank and ladle) is used to wash. The tub is not climbed into; water is ladled from the tub and splashed over the head. The traditional Asian toilet is of the squat variety. (Toilets are called *kamar kecil* – the universal 'small room' – or *way say*, as in the initials 'WC'.) Toilet paper is not traditionally used; the faithful left hand and water suffice. In cheaper accommodation you are expected to bring your own towels, soap and toilet paper.

Eating and drinking → *For restaurant price codes, see box, above.*

Food

The main staple across the archipelago is rice. Today, alternatives such as corn, sweet potatoes and sago, which are grown primarily in the dry islands of the East, are regarded as 'poor man's food', and rice is the preferred staple.

Indonesians will eat rice – or *nasi* (milled, cooked rice) – at least three times a day. Breakfast is often left-over rice, stir-fried and served up as *nasi goreng*. Mid-morning snacks are often sticky rice cakes or *pisang goreng* (fried bananas). Rice is the staple for lunch, served up with two or three meat and vegetable dishes and followed by fresh fruit. The main meal is supper, which is served quite early and again consists of rice, this time accompanied by as many as five or six other dishes. *Sate/satay* (grilled skewers of meat), *soto* (a nourishing soup) or *bakmi* (noodles, a dish of Chinese origin) may be served first.

In many towns (particularly in Java), *sate, soto* or *bakmi* vendors roam the streets with carts containing charcoal braziers, ringing a bell or hitting a block (the noise will signify what he or she is selling) in the early evenings. These carts are known as *kaki lima* (five legs). *Pedagang* (vendor) *kaki lima* also refers to hawkers who peddle their wares from stalls and from baskets hung from shoulder poles.

Larger foodstalls tend to set up in the same place every evening in a central position in town. These *warungs*, as they are known, may be temporary structures or more permanent buildings, with simple tables and benches. In the larger cities, there may be an area of *warungs*, all under one roof. Often a particular street will become known as the best place to find particular dishes like *martabak* (savoury meat pancakes) or *gado gado* (vegetable salad served with peanut sauce). It is common to see some *warungs* labelled *wartegs*. These are stalls selling dishes from Tegal, a town on Java's north coast. More formalized restaurants are known simply as *rumah makan* (literally 'eating houses'), often shortened to just 'RM'. A good place to look for cheap stall food is in and around the market or *pasar*; night markets or *pasar malam* are usually better for eating than day markets.

Feast days, such as Lebaran marking the end of Ramadan, are a cause for great celebration and traditional dishes are served. *Lontong* or *ketupat* are made at this time (they are both versions of boiled rice – simmered in a small container or bag, so that as it cooks, the rice is compressed to make a solid block). This may be accompanied by *sambal goreng daging* (fried beef in a coconut sauce) in Java or *rendang* (curried beef) in Sumatra. *Nasi kuning* (yellow rice) is traditionally served at a *selamatan* (a Javanese celebration marking a birth, the collection of the rice harvest or the completion of a new house).

In addition to rice, there are a number of other common ingredients used across the country. Coconut milk, ginger, chilli peppers and peanuts are used nationwide, while dried salted fish and soybeans are important sources of protein. In coastal areas, fish and seafood tend to be more important than meat. As Indonesia is more than 80% Muslim, pork is not widely eaten (except in Chinese restaurants) but in some areas, such as Bali, Christian Flores and around Lake Toba in Sumatra, it is much more in evidence.

Regional cuisines

Although Indonesia is becoming more homogeneous as Javanese culture spreads to the Outer Islands, there are still distinctive regional cuisines. The food of Java embraces a number of regional forms, of which the most distinctive is **Sundanese**. *Lalap*, a Sundanese dish, consists of raw vegetables and is said to be the only Indonesian dish where vegetables are eaten uncooked. Characteristic ingredients of Javanese dishes are soybeans, beef, chicken and vegetables; characteristic flavours are an interplay of sweetness and spiciness. Probably the most famous regional cuisine, however, is **Padang** or **Minang** food, which has its origins in West Sumatra province. Padang food has 'colonized' the rest of the country and there are Padang restaurants in every town, no matter how small. Dishes tend to be hot and spicy, using quantities of chilli and turmeric, and include *rendang* (dry beef curry), *kalo ayam* (creamy chicken curry) and *dendeng balado* (fried seasoned sun-dried meat with a spicy coating). In **Eastern Indonesia**, seafood and fish are important elements in the diet, and fish grilled over an open brazier (*ikan panggang* or *ikan bakar*) and served with spices and rice is a delicious, common dish. The **Toraja** of Sulawesi eat large amounts of pork, and specialities include black rice (*nasi hitam*) and fish or chicken cooked in bamboo (*piong*). There are large numbers of Chinese people scattered across the archipelago and, like other countries of the region, **Chinese** restaurants are widespread.

Drink

Water must be boiled for at least five minutes before it is safe to drink. Hotels and most restaurants should boil the water they offer customers. Ask for *air minum* (drinking water). Many restaurants provide a big jug of boiled water on each table. In cheaper establishments it is probably best to play safe and ask for bottled water, although consider the environmental impact of this.

'**Mineral water**' – of which the most famous is *Aqua* ('aqua' has become the generic word for mineral water) – is available in all but the smallest and most remote towns. Check the seal is intact before accepting a bottle. Bottled water is cheap: in 2011 a 1.5 litre bottle cost around 3500Rp. Bottled water is considerably cheaper at supermarkets than at the many kiosks lining the streets.

Western **bottled and canned drinks** are widely available in Indonesia and are comparatively cheap. Alternatively, most restaurants will serve *air jeruk* (citrus **fruit juices**) with or without ice (*es*). The **coconut milk** is a good thirst quencher and a good source of potassium and glucose. Fresh fruit juices vary greatly in quality; some are little more than water, sugar and ice. Ice in many places is fine, but in cheaper restaurants and away from tourist areas many people recommend taking drinks without ice. Javanese, Sumatran, Sulawesi or Timorese *kopi* (coffee), fresh and strong, is an excellent morning pick-you-up.

It is usually served *kopi manis* (sweet) and black; if you want to have it without sugar, ask for it *tidak pakai gula*. The same goes for other drinks habitually served with mountains of sugar (like fruit juices). *Susu* (milk) is available in tourist areas and large towns, but it may be sweetened condensed milk. *Teh* (tea), usually weak, is obtainable almost everywhere. *Teh jahe* (hot ginger tea) is a refreshing alternative.

Although Indonesia is a predominantly Muslim country, alcohol is widely available. The two most popular **beers** – light lagers – are the locally brewed *Anker* and *Bintang* brands. Wine is becoming more popular. A reasonable bottle can be had for around US$15. Imported **spirits** are comparatively expensive, however, a number of local brews including *brem* (rice wine), *arak* (rice whisky) and *tuak* (palm wine) are available.

Local customs and laws

As a rule, Indonesians are courteous and understanding. Visitors should be the same. Foreigners are often given the benefit of the doubt when norms are transgressed. However, it is best to have a grasp of at least the basics of accepted behaviour. There are also some areas – such as Aceh in North Sumatra – that are more fervently Muslim than other parts of the country. With such a diverse array of cultures and religions, accepted conduct varies. Generally, the more popular an area is (as a tourist destination) the more understanding local people are likely to be of tourist habits. But this is not to imply that anything goes. It is also true that familiarity can breed contempt, so even in places like Bali it is important to be sensitive to the essentials of local culture.

Calmness Like other countries of Southeast Asia, a calm attitude is highly admired, especially if things are going wrong. Keep calm and cool when bargaining, or waiting for a delayed bus or appointment.

Dress Indonesia is largely a Muslim country. Dress modestly and avoid shorts, short skirts and sleeveless dresses or shirts (except at the beach). Public nudity and topless bathing are not acceptable. Light clothing is suitable all year round, except at night in the mountains. Proper decorum should be observed when visiting places of worship; shorts are not permitted in mosques, shoulders and arms should be covered, and women must cover their heads. Formal dress for men normally consists of a batik shirt and trousers; suits are rarely worn. Local women usually wear a *kebaya*.

Face People should not be forced to lose face in public; especially in front of colleagues. Putting someone in a position of *malu* or social shame should be avoided.

Gifts If you are invited to somebody's home, it is customary to take a gift. This is not opened until after the visitor has left. Most small general stores have a range of pre-wrapped and boxed gifts, appropriate for a variety of occasions including weddings. These are usually items of china or glasses.

Heads, hands and feet The head is considered sacred and should never be touched (especially those of children). Handshaking is common among both men and women, but the use of the left hand to give or receive is taboo. When eating with fingers, use the right hand only. Pointing with your finger is impolite; use your thumb to point. Beckon buses (or any person) with a flapping motion of your right hand down by your side. When sitting with others, do not cross your legs; it is considered disrespectful. Do not point with your feet and keep them off tables. Remove shoes when entering houses.

Open affection Public displays of affection between men and women are considered objectionable. However, Indonesians of the same sex tend to be affectionate – holding hands, for example.

Punctuality *Jam karet* or 'rubber time' is a peculiarly Indonesian phenomenon. Patience and a cool head are very important; appointments are rarely at the time arranged.

Religion Indonesia is the largest Muslim country in the world. In Java, **Islam** is a synthesis of Islam, Buddhism, Hinduism and Animism – although the extent to which it is 'syncretic' is vigorously debated. Orthodox Islam is strongest in northern Sumatra, but is also present in parts of Sulawesi, Kalimantan and West Java. Since the Bali bombings and suicide attacks in Jakarta, Islam in Indonesia, and the *pesentren* (Islamic boarding schools – the most famous being Al-Mukmin Ngruki in Java with graduates including the Bali bombers) have been put under the microscope with the government keen to disassociate itself with any links to fundamentalist groups. However, the government has so far proved itself unable to stop radical groups agitating, despite placing huge emphasis on intelligence and anti-terror schemes.

Mosques are sacred houses of prayer; non-Muslims can enter a mosque, so long as they observe the appropriate customs: remove shoes before entering, dress appropriately, do not disturb the peace, and do not walk too close to or in front of somebody who is praying. During the fasting month of Ramadan, do not eat, drink or smoke in the presence of Muslims during daylight hours.

Bali has remained a **Hindu** island, and remnants of Hinduism are also evident in parts of Central and East Java. To enter a temple or *pura* on Bali, it is often necessary to wear a sash around the waist (at some temples a sarong is also required); these are available for hire at the more popular temples, or can be bought for about 10,000Rp (20,000Rp for a sarong). Modest and tidy dress is also required when visiting Hindu temples; women should not enter wearing short dresses or with bare shoulders. Do not use flash during ceremonies. Women menstruating are requested not to enter temples.

Pockets of **Christianity** can be found throughout the archipelago, notably in East Nusa Tenggara, around Danau Toba and Sulawesi. Evangelical Christianity is enjoying large numbers of converts among the ethnic Chinese.

Indonesian festivals and events → *Muslim festivals are based on the lunar calendar.*

January
Tahun Baru, New Year's Day (1st: public holiday). **New Year's Eve** is celebrated with street carnivals, shows, fireworks and all-night festivities. In Christian areas, festivities are more exuberant, with people visiting each other on New Year's Day and attending church services.

January/February
Imlek, Chinese New Year (movable, 23 Jan 2012, 10 Feb 2013). An official holiday; many Chinese shops and businesses close for at least 2 days. Within the Chinese community, younger people visit their relatives, children are given *hong bao* (lucky money), new clothes are bought and any unfinished business is cleared up.

March/April
Garebeg Maulad, or Maulud Nabi Muhammed, birthday of the Prophet Mohammad, (movable, 4 Feb 2012, 24 Jan 2013: public holiday), to commemorate Prophet Muhammad's birthday in AD 571. Processions and Koran recitals in most big towns. Celebrations begin a week before the actual day and last a month, with *selamatans* in homes, mosques and schools.

Wafat Isa Al-Masih, Good Friday (movable, 6 Apr 2012, 29 March 2013: public holiday).
Nyepi (movable, 23 Mar 2012, 06 April 2013: public holiday). Solar New Year, which is held at the spring equinox. In the recent past it was a day of silence when everything closed down and no activity was allowed. It is hoped that the evil spirits roused by the previous night's activities will find Bali to be a barren land and will leave the island. On the day before Nyepi long parades of traditionally dressed Balinese, carrying offerings and sacred objects, walk from their villages to nearby riverbanks and beaches to undertake ritual ablutions of purification and ask for their deity's blessing. As part of

the *melasti* rites, the village gods in their *pratimas* (the small statue in which a god is invited to reside during a ceremony) are taken from the village temples and carried to the seashore for resanctification. Balinese believe that the sea will receive all evil and polluted elements, it is a place to cast off the evil words and deeds of the past year, and seek renewal and purification for the new Hindu year.

Note Visitors must stay within their hotel compounds from 0500 to 0500 the following day; the observance of Nyepi is very strict in this regard, you might choose to avoid being on the island during this time. Tourists are confined to their accommodation, which in a small guesthouse means you feel as if you have been placed under 'house arrest' – no swimming in the sea 10 m from your bungalow, no strolls or other forms of exercise. Anyone arriving at Denpasar airport on the eve of Nyepi should be aware that most taxi drivers go home at 1700. The few who continue to offer a taxi service up to midnight ask exorbitant rates and may be unlicensed. Travellers should arrange transport in advance with their accommodation.

Kartini Day (21 Apr). A ceremony held by women to mark the birthday of Raden Ajeng Kartini, born in 1879 and proclaimed as a pioneer of women's emancipation. Women are supposed to be pampered by their husbands and children, although it is women's organizations like the Dharma Wanita who get most excited. Women wear national dress.

May
Waisak Day (movable, 28 Apr 2012, 25 May 2013: public holiday). Marks the birth and death of the historic Buddha; at Candi Mendut outside Yogyakarta, a procession of monks carrying flowers, candles, holy fire and images of the Buddha walk to Borobudur.

Kenaikan Isa Al-Masih or Ascension Day (movable, 17 May 2012, 9 May 2013: public holiday).

June/July
Al Miraj or Isra Miraj Nabi Muhammed (movable, 16 Jun 2012, 5 Jun 2013). The ascension of the Prophet Mohammad when he is led through the 7 heavens by the archangel. He speaks with God and returns to earth the same night, with instructions that include the 5 daily prayers.

August
Independence Day (17 Aug: public holiday). The most important national holiday, celebrated with processions and dancing. Although it's officially on 17 Aug, festivities continue for a month, towns are decorated with bunting and parades cause delays to bus travel, there seems to be no way of knowing when each town will hold its parades.

Awal Ramadan (movable, 19 Jul 2012, 9 Jul 2013). The 1st day of Ramadan, a month of fasting for all Muslims. Muslims abstain from all food, drink and smoking from sunrise to sundown – if they are very strict, Muslims do not even swallow their own saliva during daylight hours. It is strictly adhered to in more conservative areas like Aceh and West Sumatra, and many restaurants remain closed during daylight hours – making life tiresome for non-Muslims. Every evening for 30 days before breaking of fast, stalls selling traditional Malay cakes and delicacies are set up. The only people exempt from fasting are the elderly, those who are travelling and women who are pregnant or menstruating.

September
Idul Fitri (Aidil Fitri) or **Lebaran** (movable, 18 Aug 2012, 9 Aug 2013: public holiday)

is a 2-day celebration that marks the end of Ramadan, and is a period of prayer and celebration. In order for Hari Raya to be declared, the new moon of Syawal has to be sighted; if it is not, fasting continues for another day. It is the most important time of the year for Muslim families. Mass prayers are held in mosques and squares. Public transport is booked up weeks in advance and hotels are often full.

October
Hari Pancasila (1 Oct). This commemorates the Five Basic Principles of Pancasila.
Armed Forces Day (5 Oct). The anniversary of the founding of the Indonesian Armed Forces; military parades and demonstrations.

November/December
Idhul Adha (movable, 25 Oct 2012, 15 Oct 2013: public holiday). Celebrated by Muslims to mark the 10th day of Zulhijjah, the 12th month of the Islamic calendar when pilgrims celebrate their return from the Haj to Mecca. In the morning, prayers are offered; later, families hold 'open house'. This is the 'festival of the sacrifice'. Burial graves are cleaned, and an animal is sacrificed to be distributed to the poor to commemorate the willingness of Abraham to sacrifice his son. Indonesian men who have made the pilgrimage to Mecca wear a white skull-hat.

Muharram (movable, 14 Nov 2012, 4 Nov 2013: public holiday), Muslim New Year. Marks the 1st day of the Muslim calendar and celebrates the Prophet Muhammad's journey from Mecca to Medina on the lunar equivalent of AD 16 Jul 622.
Christmas Day (25 Dec: public holiday). Celebrated by Christians – the Bataks of Sumatra, the Toraja and Minahasans of Sulawesi and in some of the islands of Nusa Tenggara, and Irian Jaya.

Shopping

Indonesia offers a wealth of distinctive handicrafts and other products. Best buys include textiles (batik and *ikat*), silverwork, woodcarving, *krisses* (indigenous daggers), puppets, paintings and ceramics. Bali has the greatest choice of handicrafts. It is not necessarily the case that you will find the best buys in the area where a particular product is made; the larger cities, especially Jakarta, sell a wide range of handicrafts and antiques from across the archipelago at competitive prices.

Tips on buying

Early morning sales may well be cheaper, as salespeople often believe the first sale augurs well for the rest of the day. Except in the larger fixed-price stores, bargaining (with good humour) is expected; start at 60% lower than the asking price. Do not expect to achieve instant results; if you walk away from the shop, you will almost certainly be followed, with a lower offer. If the salesperson agrees to your price, you should feel obliged to purchase – it is considered very ill mannered to agree on a price and then not buy the article.

What to buy

Centres of batik-making are focused on Java. Yogyakarta and Solo (Surakarta) probably offer the widest choice. There is also a good range of batik in Jakarta. The traditional hand-drawn batiks (*batik tulis*) are more expensive than the modern printed batiks. *Ikat* is dyed and woven cloth found on the islands of Bali, Lombok and Nusa Tenggara, although it is not cheap and is sometimes of dubious quality. *Wayang* is a Javanese and Balinese art form and puppets are most widely available on these islands, particularly in Yogyakarta and Jakarta. Baskets of all shapes and sizes are made for practical use, out of rattan, bamboo, sisal, and nipah and lontar palm. The intricate baskets of Lombok are particularly attractive. Woodcarving ranges from the clearly tourist oriented (Bali), to fine classical pieces (Java), to 'primitive' (Papua). The greatest concentration of woodcarvers work in Bali, producing skilful modern and traditional designs. For a more contemporary take on Indonesian fashion, head to the *distros* of Bandung for some seriously unique T-shirts and accessories.

Essentials A-Z

Accident and emergency
Ambulance T118, Fire T113, Police T110.

Customs and duty free
The duty-free allowance is 2 litres of alcohol, 200 cigarettes or 50 cigars or 100 g of tobacco, along with a reasonable amount of perfume.

Prohibited items include narcotics, arms and ammunition, pornographic objects or printed matter.

Internet
Any town of any size will have an internet café. Costs vary from 3000Rp-20,000Rp per hr. Indonesia is a surpisingly well-wired country and many hotels, cafés and even convenience stores offer Wi-Fi (though frustratingly hotels often charge for access). Smartphones, particulalarly Blackberry and their BBM (Blackberry messenger service) have taken off here in recent years.

Health
See your doctor or travel clinic at least 6 weeks before your departure for general advice on travel risks, malaria and vaccinations required for the region you are visiting. Make sure you have travel insurance, get a dental check (especially if you are going to be away for more than a month), know your own blood group and if you suffer a long-term condition such as diabetes or epilepsy make sure someone knows or that you have a Medic Alert bracelet/necklace with this information on it.

Health risks
The following covers some of the more common risks to travellers but is by no means comprehensive.

Malaria exists across the region. Always check with your doctor or travel clinic for the most up-to-date advice. Note that medicine in developing countries, in particular anti-malarials, may be sub-standard or part of a trade in counterfeit drugs. Malaria can cause death within 24 hrs. It can start as something resembling an attack of flu. You may feel tired, lethargic, headachy, feverish; or more seriously, develop fits, followed by coma and then death. Have a low index of suspicion because it is very easy to write off vague symptoms that may actually be malaria. If you have a temperature, go to a doctor as soon as you can and ask for a malaria test. On your return home if you suffer any of these symptoms, get tested as soon as possible, even if any previous test proved negative; a test could save your life.

The most serious viral disease is **dengue fever**, which is hard to protect against as the mosquitoes bite throughout the day as well as at night – use insect avoidance methods at all times. Symptoms are similar to malaria and include fever, intense joint pain and a rash. Rest, plenty of fluids and paracetamol is the best treatment.

Each year there is the possibility that **avian flu SARS** might rear their ugly heads. Check the news reports. If there is a problem in an area you are due to visit you may be advised to have an ordinary flu shot or to seek expert advice.

Rabies and **schistosomiasis** (bilharzia, a water-borne parasite) may be a problem. Be aware of the dangers of the bite from any animal. If bitten clean the wound and treat with an iodine-based disinfectant or alcohol. Always seek urgent medical attention even if you have been previously vaccinated!

Bites and stings are rare but if you are bitten by a snake, spider or scorpion, stay as calm as possible, try to identify the culprit and seek medical advice without delay.

Bacterial diseases include **tuberculosis** (TB) and some causes of traveller's diarrhoea. **Diarrhoea** is common but if symptoms persist beyond 2 weeks medical attention should be sought. Also seek medical advice if there is blood in the stools and/or fever. Keep well hydrated (rehydration sachets are invaluable) and eat bland foods. Bacterial diarrhoea is the most common; your GP may prescribe antibiotics for you to take with you. To minimize the chances of diarrhoea be careful with water (see below) and food, particularly salads, meat and unpasteurized dairy products. Where possible, watch food being prepared. There is a simple adage that says: wash it, peel it, boil it or forget it.

Typhoid is spread by the insanitary preparation of food. A number of vaccines are available, including one taken orally.

Water should be treated with iodine and filtered. Avoid tap water and ice in drinks. Check seals on bottled water are unbroken.

Take good heed of advice regarding protecting yourself against the sun. Overexposure can lead to **sunburn** and, in the longer term, skin cancers and premature skin aging. Avoid exposure to the sun by covering exposed skin, wearing a hat and staying out of the sun, particularly between late morning and early afternoon. Apply a high-factor sunscreen and also make sure it screens against UVB. A further danger in tropical climates is **heat exhaustion** or more seriously **heatstroke**. This can be avoided by good hydration, which means drinking water past the point of simply quenching thirst. Also when first exposed to tropical heat take time to acclimatize by avoiding strenuous activity in the middle of the day. If you cannot avoid heavy exercise it is also a good idea to increase salt intake.

Useful resources

www.btha.org British Travel Health Association (UK). This is the official website of an organization of travel health professionals.
www.cdc.gov US Government site that gives excellent advice on travel health and details of disease outbreaks.

www.fco.gov.uk Foreign and Commonwealth Office.
www.fitfortravel.scot.nhs.uk A-Z of vaccine/health advice for each country.
www.nathnac.org National Travel Health Network and Centre.
www.who.int The WHO Blue Book lists the diseases of the world.

Vaccinations See you doctor or a specialist travel clinic 6-8 weeks before travel for advice. The following vaccinations are usually advised before travel to Southeast Asia: BCG, diphtheria, hepatitis A, polio, tetanus and typhoid. The following are sometimes advised before travel to Southeast Asia: hepatitis B, Japanese B encephalitis, tuberculosis and rabies. A yellow fever vaccination certificate is required if coming from areas with risk of transmission. If you have been travelling in Africa or South America in a country in the yellow-fever zone within 6 days of arriving in Southeast Asia check to see if you require proof of vaccination.

Language

The national language is Bahasa Indonesia, which is written in Roman script. There are 250 regional languages and dialects, of which Sundanese (the language of West Java and Jakarta) is the most widespread. In Padang and elsewhere in West Sumatra, the population speak Minang, which is also similar to Bahasa. About 70% of the population can speak Bahasa. English is the most common foreign language, with some Dutch and Portuguese speakers.

Bahasa Indonesia is relatively easy to learn, a small number of useful words and phrases are listed in the box, above.

The best way to learn Indonesian is to study it intensively in Indonesia. In Jakarta and Bali, a variety of short and long courses (including homestay programmes in Bali) are available through **The Indonesia-Australia Language Foundation (IALF)**, T021 521 3350, www.ialf.edu. In Yogyakarta, another centre where overseas students study Indonesian, courses are run by the **Realia Language School**, T0274 583229, www.realians.com, which is recommended. It is cheaper if a group learns together.

Money → *US$1 = 8836Rp, £1 = 13,940Rp, €1 = 12,197Rp (Oct 2011)*

The unit of currency in Indonesia is the rupiah (Rp). When taking US$ in cash, make sure the bills are new and crisp, as banks in Indonesia can be fussy about which bills they accept (Flores and Sumatra are particularly bad). Larger denomination US$ bills also tend to command a premium exchange rate. In more out of the way places it is worth making sure that you have a stock of smaller notes and coins – it can be hard to break larger bills.

Two of the better banks are **Bank Negara Indonesia (BNI)** and **Bank Central Asia (BCA)**. BNI is reliable and efficient and most of their branches will change US$ TCs. Banks in larger towns and tourist centres have ATMs. Cash or traveller's cheques (TCs) can be changed in most tourist centres at a competitive rate. Credit cards are widely accepted.

Tipping is commonplace in Indonesia, and small bills are often handed over at the end of every transaction to smooth it over and ensure good service. Indeed, it can often seem that the whole country is founded on tipping, an informal way of channelling money through society so that lower earners can supplement their meagre earnings and are motivated into action. A 10% service charge is added to bills at more expensive hotels. Porters expect to be tipped about 2000Rp a bag. In more expensive restaurants, where no service is charged, a tip of 5-10% may be appropriate. Taxi drivers (in larger towns) appreciate a small tip (1000Rp). *Parkirs* always expect payment for 'watching' your vehicle; 1000Rp.

Cost of travelling

Indonesia is no longer the bargain country it was 10 years ago. Whilst it is still cheap by Western standards tourists can now expect to dig deeper for their meals and accommodation. Visitors staying in 1st-class hotels and eating in top-notch restaurants will probably spend between US100 and US$150 a day. Tourists on a mid-range budget, staying in cheaper a/c accommodation and eating in local restaurants, will probably spend between US$50-80 a day. A backpacker, staying in fan-cooled guesthouses and eating cheaply, could scrape by on US$20-25 a day, though this leaves little room for wild partying. Indonesia has seen prices spiral in recent years, particularly for food and this is reflected in the increased costs that travellers now have to bear when visiting the country.

Post

The postal service is relatively reliable; though important mail should be registered. Every town and tourist centre has either a *kantor pos* (post office) or postal agent, where you can buy stamps, post letters and parcels.

Safety

Despite the recent media coverage of terrorist plots and attacks, riots and other disturbances in Indonesia, it remains a safe country and violence against foreigners is rare. Petty theft is a minor problem.

Avoid carrying large amounts of cash; TCs can be changed in most major towns.

Beware of the confidence tricksters who are widespread in tourist areas. Sudden reports of unbeatable bargains or closing down sales are usual ploys.

Civil unrest The following areas of Indonesia have seen disturbances in recent years and visits are not recommended: Maluku (around Ambon), Central Sulawesi (around Palu and Poso). Both these places have been victims of sectarian violence.

However, these incidents have been localized and almost never affected foreign visitors. Embassies ask visitors to exercise caution when travelling in Aceh, a region recovering from a long internal conflict.

Flying After a series of accidents the EU banned many Indonesian airlines from entering its air space over continuing concerns of poor maintenance and safety. The Indonesian government and airline companies have taken this very seriously and the last few years have seen brand new Boeings and Airbuses being rolled out by Lion Air and Garuda. The airlines considered acceptable by the EU are Batavia, Garuda and Indonesia AirAsia. Many European embassies advise against domestic air travel. For the latest information, see www.fco.gov.uk/en and www.travel.state.gov/travel/warnings.html.

Telephone → *Country code +62.*
Operator T101. International enquiries T102. Local enquiries T108. Long-distance enquiries T106. Every town has its communication centres (Wartel), where you can make local and international calls and faxes.

Mobile phones Known as hand-phones or HP in Indonesia, use has sky rocketed and costs are unbelievably low. It usually costs around 15,000Rp to buy a Sim card with a number. Top-up cards are sold at various denominations. If you buy a 10,000Rp or 20,000Rp card, the vendor will charge a few more thousand, in order to gain some profit. If you buy a 100,000Rp card, you will pay a few thousand less than 100,000Rp. This is standard practice throughout the country. Beware of vendors in Kuta, Bali who try and sell Sim cards at highly inflated prices. Reliable operators include Telkomsel, IM3 and Pro XL. If you want to buy a dirt cheap phone in country, look for the Esia brand which offers bargain basement phone and credit packages.

Tax
Expect to pay 11% tax in the more expensive restaurants, particularly in tourist areas of Bali and Lombok. Some cheaper restaurants serving foreigners may add 10% to the bill.

Airport tax 75,000Rp-150,000Rp on international flights (Jakarta and Denpasar are both 150,000Rp), and anywhere between 10,000Rp and 30,000Rp on domestic flights, depending on the airport.

Visas and immigration
Visitors from several nations, including Malaysia, The Philippines and Singapore are allowed a visa-free stay of 30 days in Indonesia. Visitors from nations including the following are able to get a US$25 30-day **Visa On Arrival (VOA)**: Australia, Canada, France, Germany, Holland, Ireland, Italy, New Zealand, Portugal, Spain, United Kingdom and the USA. Check with your embassy. Pay at a booth at the port of entry. These visas are extendable at immigration offices in the country for an extra 30 days. In Bali many travel agents offer to extend visas, for a fee. Visitors wishing to obtain a VOA must enter and leave Indonesia though certain ports of entry, including the following:
Sea ports Batam, Tanjung Uban, Belawan (Medan), Dumai, Jayapura, Tanjung Balaikarimun, Bintang Pura (Tanjung Pinang), and Kupang.
Airports Medan, Pekanbaru, Padang, Jakarta, Surabaya, Bali, Manado, Adisucipto in Yogyakarta, Adisumarmo in Solo, and Selaparang in Mataram, Lombok.

A US$10 VOA (7 days) is available for visitors to the Riau islands of Batam and Bintan.

60-day visitor visas (B211) are available at Indonesian embassies and consulates around the world (a ticket out of the country, 2 photos and a completed visa form is necessary). Costs vary. They can be extended giving a total stay of 6 months (must be extended at an immigration office in Indonesia each month after the initial 60-day visa has expired; take it to the office 4 days before expiry). To extend the visa in Indonesia, a fee of US$25 is levied and a sponsor letter from a local person is needed. To obtain a 60-day visitor visa in Singapore, a one-way ticket from Batam to Singapore is adequate: purchase from the ferry centre at HarbourFront in Singapore.

It is crucial to check this information before travelling as the visa situation in Indonesia is extremely volatile. Travellers who overstay their visa will be fined US$20 a day. Long-term overstayers can expect a fine and jail sentence. See www.indonesianembassy. org.uk for more information.

All visitors to Indonesia must possess a passport valid for at least 6 months from their date of arrival in Indonesia, and they should have proof of onward travel. It is not uncommon for immigration officers to ask to see a ticket out of the country. (A Batam–Singapore ferry ticket or cheap Medan–Penang air ticket will suffice).

Denpasar

Once the royal capital of the princely kingdom of Badung, there is little evidence now of Denpasar's past. Situated in the south of the island, about 5 km from the coast, Bali's capital has grown in the past 10-15 years from a sleepy village to a bustling city with choked streets buzzing with the sound of waspish motorbikes. Today, the town has a population of over 450,000 and is Bali's main trade and transport hub, with its central business area centred around Jalan Gajah Mada. Puputan Square pays homage to the tragic end of the Rajah and his court; it is named after the 'battle to the death' – or puputan – against a force of Dutch soldiers in 1906.

Ins and outs → *Phone code: 0361.*

Getting there

Denpasar's **Ngurah Rai International Airport** ① *24-hr airport information T0361 22238, flight information T0361 7571647, at the south end of the island, just south of Kuta,* is one of Indonesia's 'gateways', with regular international connections with Southeast Asian cities and beyond. It also has excellent domestic connections. International departure tax is 150,000Rp; domestic is 30,000Rp. A tourist office with a well-run hotel booking counter offers comprehensive details and prices of upmarket accommodation on Bali. Other facilities include money changers, ATMs, bars, restaurant, shops and taxi counter.

There are fixed-price taxis from the airport, starting at US$4.50; US$5 to Kuta 2; US$5.50 to Legian and US$6 to Seminyak; US$19.50 to Ubud; US$33.50 to Padangbai and US$33.50 to Candi Dasa. Alternatively, catch a cab just after it has dropped someone off at the International Departures area. This is a little cheeky, but the drivers use the meter and the cost of the drive to Kuta is around US$3.50. Some hardened souls walk all the way along the beach towards Tuban or Kuta.

Getting around

As Bali's capital, Denpasar is well connected with the rest of the island. No fewer than five terminals provide bemo services and minibuses run between the different terminals. Metered taxis are also abundant in Denpasar.

Tourist information

The **tourist office** ① *Jln Surapati 7, T0361 223602, Mon-Thu 0730-1530, Fri 0730-1300,* is not utilized very often, which is a shame given the eagerness of the staff. The office provides a free map, calendar of events and Bali brochure.

Sights → *For listings, see pages 23-25.*

Denpasar is not particularly attractive and the major tourist attraction is easily found in the centre of town and is a focus for local hawkers. The **Museum Bali** ① *T0361 222680, Mon-Thu 0800-1500, Fri 0800-1230, Sat 0800-1500, 2000Rp, child 1000Rp,* was established in 1931 and is situated on the east side of Puputan Square. The entrance is on Jalan Mayor Wismu. The museum, built in 1910, mirrors the architecture of Balinese temples and palaces, and is contained within a series of attractive courtyards with well-kept gardens. The impressive collection of pre-historic artefacts, sculpture, masks, textiles, weaponry and contemporary arts and crafts was assembled with the help of Walter Spies, the German artist who made Bali his home. Labelling could be better and there is no guide. Nonetheless, it gives an impression of the breadth of the island's culture.

Next door to the museum is the new **Pura Jaganatha**, a temple dedicated to the Supreme God *Sang Hyang Widi Wasa*. The statue of a turtle and two nagas signify the foundation of the world. The complex is dominated by the *Padma Sana* or lotus throne, upon which the gods sit. The central courtyard is surrounded by a moat filled with water-lilies and the most enormous carp.

From an archaeological perspective, **Pura Masopahit** is the most important temple in Denpasar. The main gateway to the **pura** faces the main street, but the entrance is down a side road off the west end of Jalan Tabanan. The temple is one of the oldest in Bali, probably dating from the introduction of Javanese civilization from Majapahit in the 15th century, after which it is named. It was badly damaged during the 1917 earthquake, but has since been partly restored. Note the fine reconstructed split gate, with its massive figures of a giant and a garuda.

The **Taman Werdi Budaya Art Centre** ① *Jln Nusa Indah, Tue-Sun 0800-1700, free,* was established in 1973 to promote Balinese visual and performing arts. It contains an open-air auditorium, along with three art galleries. Arts and crafts are also sold here. Activity peaks during the annual **Bali Festival of Art**, held from mid-June for a month.

Denpasar listings

For Sleeping and Eating price codes and other relevant information, see pages 7-10.

⊜ Sleeping

Denpasar *p22*
Most people head to the beach areas in southern Bali, which are closer to the airport. Accommodation in Denpasar is geared more towards the domestic market and can get busy during holidays.
$$$ Inna Hotel, Jln Veteran 3, T0361 225681, www.innabali.com. Built in the 1930s, this was the first hotel on Bali. Its glory has somewhat faded, but pockets of charm remain. Clean rooms, pool and a garden.

$$ Adinda Hotel, Jln Karma 8, T0361 249435. The superior rooms are huge, bright and have bath and TV. Standard rooms are a little pokey, and have tiny windows. Garden.
$$ Hotel Taman Suci, Jln Imam Bonjol 45, T0361 484445, www.tamansuci.com. Near Tegal bemo station, with spacious clean rooms, TV and minibar. De luxe rooms have bath.

⊙ Eating

Denpasar *p22*
Indonesian food dominates the scene. There is a collection of clean *warungs* outside the Inna Hotel selling Indonesian favourites.

$ Aseupan, Jln Tukad Unda 7, Renon, T0361 743 1501. Sundanese food served in clean, simple restaurant. Recommended.

$ Mie 88, Jln Sumatra. Good range of juices and local food. Noodles are the speciality.

⊙ Shopping

Denpasar *p22*
Department stores Duta Plaza, Jln Dewi Sartika; Tiara Dewata and Matahari both have a wide range of goods. The former also has a public swimming pool.

▲ Activites and tours

Denpasar *p22*
Language schools
IALF, Jln Raya Sesetan 190, T0361 225245, ialfbali@ialf.edu. Bahasa Indonesia courses mainly suited to expats. However, they have a 2-week homestay programme combining language studies with cultural studies for AUS$1120.

⊖ Transport

Denpasar *p22*
As Denpasar is the transport hub of the island, it's easy to get to most of the main towns, beaches and sights from here.

Air
There are plenty of airline offices outside the Domestic Departures area of the airport, including AirAsia (T0804 133 3333, 0900-1700) Garuda (T0804 180 7807, 0600-0130), and Merpati (T0361 751011, 0600-1830) Transnusa (T0361 787 7555, 0600-1800).

Airline offices Batavia, Jln Teuku Umar 208-210, T0361 254947; Garuda, Jln Sugianyar 5, T0361 254747; Merpati, Jln Melati 51, T0361 235358.

Bemo
Bemos travel between the main bemo terminals (6000Rp), criss-crossing town. It is also possible to charter these bemos.

From the terminals, of which there are several, bemos travel to all of Bali's main towns: the **Ubung terminal**, north of town on Jln Cokroaminoto for trips to **West Bali**, **North Bali** and **Java**; Tegal terminal, west of town, near the intersection of Jln Imam Bonjol and Jln G Wilis, for journeys to **South Bali**; Suci terminal, near the intersection of Jln Diponegoro and Jln Hasanuddin, for **Benoa Port**; Kereneng terminal, at the east edge of town off Jln Kamboja (Jln Hayam Wuruk), for destinations around town and for **Sanur**; and Batubulan terminal, east of town just before the village of Batubulan on the road to Gianyar, for buses running **East** and to **Central Bali**. Tegal, the bemo terminal for Kuta, used to be a thriving place with crowded bemos leaving regularly. Nowadays, however, it is a shadow of its former self and you might find yourself waiting around for a while before your bemo is ready to leave. Getting the correct fare can be a challenge. Ask one of the guys at the entrance to the station who record each departure. Fares from Tegal include **Kuta**, 10000Rp; and **Sanur**, 10000Rp. Beware of pickpockets on bemos.

Due to terrible traffic congestion, bemos have been banned from Jln Legian and the road from Kuta to Seminyak is mercifully free of them.

Bus
There are also bus connections with **Java** from the Ubung terminal, just north of Denpasar on Jln Cokroaminoto.

Express and night bus offices are concentrated near the intersection of Jln Diponegoro and Jln Hasanuddin; for example, Safari Dharma Raya, Jln Diponegoro 110, T0361 231206. Journey time and fares for night and express buses include: **Jakarta**, 24 hrs, US$35; **Solo**, 18 hrs, US$25; **Yogyakarta**, 18 hrs, US$25; and **Probolinggo**, 8 hrs US$15.

Car hire

Car hire can be arranged through hotels, or one of the rental agencies in town, for approximately US$11 per day. There are also private cars (with drivers) that can be chartered by the hour or day, or for specific journeys. Bargain hard, expect to pay about US$35-50 per day (car plus driver). Drivers can be found along Jln Legian with their constant offers of transport.

Motorbike hire

Arrange hire through travel agents, hotels or from operations on the street, from 50,000Rp per day.

Ojek

Motorbike taxis, the fastest way around town, are identified by the riders' red jackets (6000Rp min).

Taxi

Numerous un-metered cars can be chartered by the hour or day, or hired for specific journeys. Bargain hard. There are also some metered taxis; the best company to use is the blue Bali Taxi, T0361 701111. Praja Bali Taxi, pale blue taxis, also operate with meters and make no extra charge for call-out service, T0361 289090. Flag fall is 5000Rp.

ℹ Directory

Denpasar *p22*

Banks BCA, Jln Mohammad Yasin, T0361 235092; Mandiri, Jln Suroprati 15, T0361 238083. **Embassies and consulates** Australia (also represents Canada, New Zealand and Papua New Guinea), Jln Hayam Wuruk 88, T0361 241118, bali@congen.dfat.gov.au. Japan, Jln Raya Puputan, Renon Denpasar 170, T0361 227628, konjdps@indo.net.id. USA, Jln Hayam Wuruk 188, T0361 233605, amcobali@indo.net.id. **Medical services** Emergency dental clinic: Jln Pattimura 19, T0361 222445. Hospitals: Sanglah Public Hospital, Jln Kesehatan Selatan 1, T0361 227911. Wangaya Hospital, Jln Kartini, T0361 222141; 24 hr on-call doctor and ambulance, Jln Cokroaminoto 28, T0361 426393. Main hospital with best emergency service. Some staff speak English. Bali's only decompression chamber for divers is located here. Bear in mind that medical facilities are not up to Western standards. For any serious medical problem, Singapore is the best place to go. **Post office** Jln Raya Puputan, Renon. Open 0800-1400 Mon-Thu, 0800-1200 Fri, 0800-1300 Sat. Poste Restante available.

South Bali

Most visitors to Bali stay in one of the resorts at the south end of the island. Most famous is Kuta, the original backpackers' haven, together with its northern extension, Legian; both of these are fairly noisy, crowded, downmarket resorts. Much nicer is Seminyak, further north, which is still relatively rural. To the south of Kuta is Tuban, a town with many hotels and restaurants. Sanur is on Bali's east coast and offers largely mid-range accommodation, though some newer budget places to stay have opened. Serangan, or Turtle Island, is a short distance offshore.

Kuta and around → *For listings, see pages 33-45. Phone code: 0361.*

Kuta was the main port and arrival point for foreigners visiting south Bali for over 100 years, from early in the 18th century, until the airport at Denpasar usurped its role. The town prospered as a hub of the slave trade in the 1830s, attracting an international cross-section of undesirables.

Miguel Covarrubias wrote in 1937 that Kuta and Sanur were "small settlements of fishermen who brave the malarial coasts". It was not until the 1960s that large numbers of Western travellers 'discovered' Kuta. Since then, it has grown into a highly developed beach resort with a mind-boggling array of hotels, restaurants and shops. While Sanur is no longer a backpackers' haven, there are still many cheap *losmen* in Kuta as well as a growing number of mid- to high-range options. Central Kuta was decimated by the Bali bombings (see box, page 30), and the area acted as a barometer for the island's suffering, with many businesses forced out of action. Things now are returning to normal, and bars such as the rebuilt **Paddies** (destroyed in the 2002 bombing) are pulling in big crowds of pleasure-hungry punters once more. Kuta's image as a beachside paradise was somewhat tarnished in early March 2011 when half the beach was closed to swimmers for a number of days due to contamination of the sea, which turned an English Channel pale brown due to all the dead plankton – a shocking shift away from its usual glassy blue.

Ins and outs

Traffic in Kuta frequently comes to a standstill, despite the one-way system. The main street, containing most of Kuta's shops, is Jalan Legian, which runs north–south (traffic travels one-way south). Jalan Pantai meets Jalan Legian at 'Bemo Corner' and is the main east–west road to the south end of the beach (with traffic going one-way west). The beach road is northbound only. There is also a government **Tourist Information Office** ① *Jl Bakungsari, T0361 756176, daily 0800-1300, 1500-1800.*

The town

Many people dislike Kuta. Other than the beach, it is not an attractive place. However, it does offer a wide range of consumerist and hedonist treats and people often find themselves staying here longer than expected. In the rainy season the drainage system is hopelessly inadequate, and some areas of Kuta, noticeably Jalan Legian, become flooded.

Since the Bali bombings, which slowed business down considerably in the area, tourists have increasingly complained of hassle from Javanese hawkers along Jalan Legian and Jalan Pantai Kuta who can get a little aggressive at times. There are also numerous women offering massage of a dubious nature on Jalan Legian. Pickpockets are less of a problem than they used to be, and children now swarm in packs selling friendship bracelets rather than rifling through your bag.

The beach

Kuta has a fine beach: a broad expanse of golden sand where local officials have taken reasonable steps to limit the persistence of hawkers. It is because of its accessibility that it is popular with surfers, although better waves can be found elsewhere. It is an excellent spot for beginners and recreational surfers. Boards can be hired on the beach and locals will offer insider knowledge of surf conditions. Strong and irregular currents can make swimming hazardous so look out for the warning notices and coloured flags that indicate which areas are safe for swimming on any particular day: red flags represent danger; yellow and red flags represent safe areas for swimming. The currents change daily and

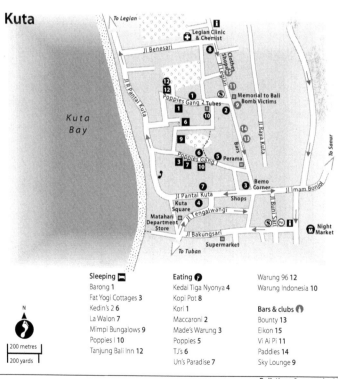

Kuta

N
200 metres
200 yards

Sleeping	Eating	Warung 96 **12**
Barong **1**	Kedai Tiga Nyonya **4**	Warung Indonesia **10**
Fat Yogi Cottages **3**	Kopi Pot **8**	
Kedin's 2 **6**	Kori **1**	**Bars & clubs**
La Walon **7**	Maccaroni **2**	Bounty **13**
Mimpi Bungalows **9**	Made's Warung **3**	Eikon **15**
Poppies I **10**	Poppies **5**	Vi Ai Pi **11**
Tanjung Bali Inn **12**	TJ's **6**	Paddies **14**
	Un's Paradise **7**	Sky Lounge **9**

there are teams of lifeguards keeping an eye on proceedings who won't hesitate to blow their whistle if they see people straying into dangerous waters. There are allegations that levels of contamination in the sea are above internationally accepted safety levels, though many people swim with no apparent ill effects.

The sand is white to the south, but grey further north. The hawkers are less of a problem now they are forbidden to cross an invisible line that divides the beach. Sit on the half of the beach closest to the sea if you want to avoid hassle. The beach faces west, so is popular at sunset, which can be truly spectacular. Head to the stretch of beach between Legian and Seminyak for cheap beachside cafés offering icy beer and glorious sunset views. On a clear day and looking north it is possible to see Gunung Agung soaring to the heavens. Religious ceremonies sometimes take place on the beach and are fascinating to watch.

Legian → *Phone code: 0361*

It is hard to say where Kuta ends and Legian begins as the main shopping street, Jalan Legian, dominates both places. Like Kuta, Legian is a shopping haven. However, Legian is far more relaxed and less congested than Kuta and there are significantly fewer hawkers.

Seminyak → *Phone code: 0361*

This area to the north of Legian begins at Jalan Double Six and runs northwards into unspoilt ricefields. With a fabulous coastline, spectacular sunsets and views of the mountains of North Bali on a clear day, it is still relatively quiet compared to Kuta and Legian, but some long-term residents are complaining that the place has lost its charm in recent years and are selling up. In August, Seminyak's villas are filled with European holidaymakers. There is good surfing, but be warned: the sea here can be lethal. There are strong undercurrents and riptides. Lifeguards patrol the beach, which is wide, sandy and much less crowded, with a few mostly mid-range to upmarket hotels dotted along it. Jalan Pura Bagus Taruna is also known as Rum Jungle Road. Jalan Dhyana Pura is also known as Jalan Abimanyu.

Travelling north from Seminyak, you pass through **Petitenget** with its large temple made of white coral (covered in moss, so not looking white at all). Further north still, the village of **Batubelig** is in an undeveloped area, with a luxury hotel and a small guesthouse. This is a surfing rather than swimming beach. Unless you are a keen walker, you will probably need to hire a car if staying in this area.

Canggu

This area of coastline, only 20 minutes north of Legian, is slowly being developed and (at the moment) offers peace and rural tranquillity, traditional villages untouched by tourism, and frequent ceremonies and festivals at one of its many temples or on the beach.

Canggu district offers unspoilt, grey-sand beaches, with the possibility of excellent surfing (easy 1- to 2-m-high waves off left- and right-hand reef breaks), as well as swimming. The following beaches are all part of Canggu: **Pererean**, **Banjartengah**, **Canggu**, **Tegal Gundul**, **Padang Linjong**, **Batu Bulong** and **Berewa**. The villages from which the beaches draw their names are inland and most offer simple homestays; just ask around. Local people are very friendly and helpful.

The drive to Canggu is very beautiful as you pass endless lush green paddy fields, coconut and banana palms, cows grazing, and the occasional picturesque, small village full of temples and shrines.

Legian & Seminyak

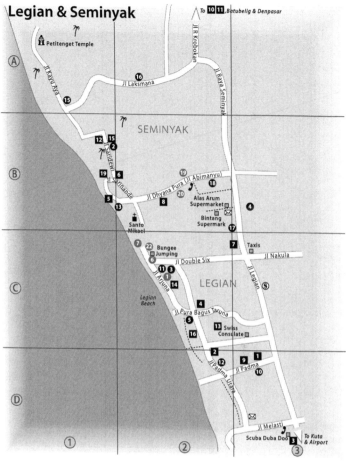

To **10** **11**, Batubelig & Denpasar

Sleeping

Sleeping 🛏

All Seasons **2** D2
Anantara **5** B1
Balisani Suites **10** A2
Bali Sorgowi **3** D3
Batubelig Beach
 Bungalows **11** A2

Casa Padma Suites **9** D3
Elsyian **12** B1
Green Room **8** B2
Island Bali **13** C2
Le Jardin **6** B2
Lokha **1** D3
O-CE-N Bali **14** C2
Puri Cendana **15** B1
Puri Raja **16** C2
Sarinande Beach Inn **19** B1
Sinar Bali **4** C2
Sun Island **7** C3

Eating 🍴

Art Café **2** B1
Café Marzano **3** C2
Gado Gado **13** B2
Indonational **10** D3
Ku De Ta **15** A1
Lanai **1** C2
Pantarei **17** B3
Seaside **11** C2
Trattoria **16** A2
Unico **4** B3
Wali Warung **5** C2
Warung Yogya **12** D2

Zula Vegetarian
 Paradise **18** B2

Bars & clubs 🍸

Bush Telegraph Pub **19** B2
Cocoon **6** C2
Dejavu **1** C2
Double Six **22** C2
Sandpit **7** C2
Q Bar **20** B2

Bali bombs

On 12 October 2002, Indonesia witnessed its most deadly terrorist attack as suicide bombers detonated near simultaneous explosions outside the **Sari Club** and **Paddies' Bar** in Kuta. The clubs and surrounding buildings were ripped to pieces by the explosions, which took the lives of 202 people, including 88 Australians and 38 Indonesians. In all, citizens of 22 countries lost their lives and many more were terribly injured. Tourists stayed away after this, causing serious damage to the economy.

As tourists began to trickle back, terrorists struck again killing 20 people on 1 October 2005 in explosions in a restaurant in Kuta square, and by beachside *warungs* in Jimbaran.

The island's tourist industry suffered immensely in the aftermath, and many places remain relatively quiet compared to the late 1990s. However, the Balinese are a resilient people, and are quietly attracting visitors to the island in numbers not seen since the blasts. While there are still fewer tourists from countries such as Britain and Australia, nationals of emerging economies such as Russia and China are almost filling the breach.

There is a well-tended memorial on Jalan Legian, Kuta, on the site of the old Paddies' Bar commemorating those who lost their lives, and opposite is **Ground Zero**, site of the Sari Club, which stands empty, although local authorities are planning a peace park.

Berewa beach

A very peaceful location (the drive from Kuta takes about 30-45 minutes; as yet there is no coast road) with an unspoilt beach backing onto ricefields, friendly local people and few tourists. There are a few unpretentious restaurants hoping to attract tourists from the local hotels; outside the high season, these are usually only open for dinner. There are also a few small shops near the hotels. The main temple is **Pura Dang Khayangan**; there has been a temple here since the 16th century. **Note** Swimming in the sea here can be dangerous.

Sanur → *For listings, see pages 33-45. Phone code: 0361.*

The first of Bali's international resorts, Sanur falls midway between the elegant, upmarket Nusa Dua and the frenetic, youthful Kuta and is situated 6 km from Denpasar. Attracting a more sedate, middle-aged clientele, many on package tours, Sanur's attractions are its long golden beach, restaurants and shopping. This is also a centre for watersports with surfing, snorkelling by Serangan Island and diving. Noticeably more expensive than Kuta, hotels tend to be mid-range to upmarket, though there are some more reasonably priced small guesthouses. Nightlife here does not compare to that of Kuta, although there are plenty of good restaurants and a few fun bars. The road parallel to the beach is lined with money changers, tourist shops (selling clothing and jewellery), tour companies, car rental outlets and shipping agents.

Sights

The **Le Mayeur Museum** ⓘ *Jln Hang Tuah, T0361 286201, Mon-Thu and Sat 0800-1500, Fri 0800-1200, 5000Rp, 2000Rp child*, is just to the north of the **Bali Beach Hotel** and is named after the famous Belgian artist Adrien Yean Le Mayeur, who arrived in Bali in 1932. He was

Sanur

Sleeping 🛏
Gazebo Cottages **3**
La Taverna **5**
Little Pond Homestay **7**
Pondok Ayu **1**
Scape Condotel **6**
Segara Village **4**
Swastika Bungalows **9**
Tanjung Sari **10**
Villa Dampati **11**
Yulia's **2**

Eating 🍴
Beach Café **1**
Benno's **1**
Cafe Batujimbar **2**
Mango Beach **1**
Manik Organik **7**
Porch **4**
Rasa Senang **5**
Sanur Rasa **8**
Smorga's **3**
Spike's Downtown Café **6**
Street Café **10**
Tambungan **9**
Village Cucine Italiana **9**

Bars & clubs 🍸
Cat & Fiddle **13**
Jimmy's Café **11**
Lazer Sports Bar **14**
Wicked Parrot **12**

immediately captivated by the culture and beauty of the island, made Sanur his home, married local beauty Ni Polok in 1935 and died in 1958. The museum contains his collection of local artefacts and some of Le Mayeur's work. The interior is dark and rather dilapidated, making the pieces difficult to view – a great shame because Le Mayeur's impressionistic works are full of tropical sunlight and colour. Le Mayeur's paintings were a great influence on a number of Balinese artists, including the highly regarded I Gusti Nyoman Nodya.

Temples made of coral are dotted along Sanur beach. The presence of primitive, pyramid-shaped structures at many of these temples suggests their origin dates back to pre-historic times. At the southern, south-facing end of Sanur beach is the **Pura Mertasari**, a small temple under a canopy of trees that is considered to harbour exceptionally powerful forces of black magic. The *odalan* festival of this temple falls at the most favoured time in the Balinese calendar, two weeks after the spring equinox. An unusual ritual trance dance, the *baris cina* (Chinese dance), is performed on the night of the festival. The dancers wear old Dutch army helmets and bayonets and the evening can end with a dramatically violent dance movement. A nearby village, **Singhi**, is home to the Black Barong, the most powerful Barong (masked figure) in Bali, made from the black feathers of a sacred rare bird.

On a clear day there are fantastic views of several mountain ranges to the north, including Gunung Agung and Gunung Batur, especially beautiful at sunset and sunrise. There is a path running along the beach for the entire length of Sanur. The beach varies in width along its length and is at its best in front of the the **Tanjung Sari** and adjacent hotels, and at the southern end. There are several roads and tracks leading down to the beach from Jalan Danau Tamblingan along its length, including Jalan Pantai Karang, where the German consul is situated, and Jalan Segara Ayu.

Serangan Island

Serangan Island is also known as Turtle Island and is, unsurprisingly, famous for its turtles. They are caught in the surrounding sea, raised in pens, and then slaughtered for their meat – which explains why they are becoming rarer by the year. The formerly common green turtle is now said to be virtually extinct in the area.

The beaches on the east coast of the island are best, with offshore coral providing good snorkelling. One of Bali's most important coastal temples is the **Pura Sakenan** in Sakenan village, at the north end of the island. Pura Sakenan's *odalan* or **anniversary festival**, held at Kuningan (the 210th day of the Balinese calendar), is thought by many to be one of the best on Bali.

Ins and outs

Boats can be chartered from Sanur. Jukungs, the brightly coloured fishing boats scattered along the beach, can be chartered by the hour (US$40) with a captain. Usually visitors leave from a jetty just south of Kampong Mesigit and 2 km southwest of Sanur; from here there are public boats to Serangan Island. Unfortunately tourists are often forced to charter a boat for far more; share if possible and bargain furiously. It is easier, and often just as cheap, to go on a tour. It is also possible to wade out to the island at low tide.

South Bali listings

For Sleeping and Eating price codes and other relevant information, see pages 7-10.

⊟ Sleeping

Kuta *p26, map p27*

It's advisable to book accommodation during the peak periods of Jul and Aug and at Christmas and New Year, as hotels are often full. There are countless places to stay. Taxi drivers are often reluctant to drive down Poppies Gangs I and II. Except when the area is flooded during the rainy season, Poppies Gang II is driveable, so it is worth trying to find a driver who will drop you by your chosen accommodation. Prices include 21% government tax and breakfast unless stated.

$$$ Barong Hotel, Poppies Gang 2, T0361 751804, www.barongbalihotel. com. In the heart of the action on Poppies Gang 2, the a/c rooms here are clean and reasonably sized. The draw is the large pool with swim-up bar and massage service. Popular with famlies.

$$$ Poppies I, Poppies Gang I, PO Box 3378, T0361 751059, www.poppiesbali.com. Running since 1973, tasteful Balinese-style a/c cottages set in beautifully landscaped gardens with pool. This peaceful and well-run hotel is very popular so book in advance.

$$ Fat Yogi Cottages and Restaurant Poppies Gang 1, T0361 751665, www.fat yogicottages.baliklik.com. Good selection of comfortable and spacious rooms some with a/c and hot water, pool. Staff can be surly.

$$ La Walon Hotel, Poppies Gang 1, T0361 757234, www.lawalonhotel.com. A spanking new exterior leads into an older wing with simple clean rooms with a/c and TV, or fan, with bathroom. Pool. Discounts available for stays of more than 1 week. Friendly staff.

$$-$ Tanjung Bali Inn, Poppies Gang 2, T0361 762990. Surrounding a swimming pool are 3 big Balinese-style buildings. Clean, large a/c and a fan rooms with

dimly lit balcony and private bathroom. Very popular.

$ Kedin's 2, Gang Sorga (off Poppies Gang 1), T0361 763554. Fan rooms with private cold-water bathroom lead onto private veranda. Pool. Warm and friendly staff, popular and relaxing hotel. Recommended.

$ Mimpi Bungalows, Gang Sorga (just off Poppies Gang 1), T0361 751848, kumimpi@ yahoo.com.sg. Simple a/c and fan rooms with hot water. Pool.

Legian *p28, map p29*

There is less budget accommodation available in Legian, but mid-range accommodation is good value here.

$$$$ O-CE-N Bali by Outrigger, Jln Arjuna 88, T0361 737 4000, www.outrigger. com. Occupying a prime piece of land overlooking the beach, this top end hotel is ultra-stylish, with sleek modern rooms, sea-view pools and jacuzzi. Strictly for surfers leading a double life as investment bankers. Discounts available. Recommended.

$$$$-$$$ Hotel Puri Raja, Jln Padma Utara, T0361 755902, www.puriraja. com. Relaxing hotel of pools and verdant gardens with sparkling white tiled rooms and access to the beach. Those who are in a sporting mood can enjoy the table tennis table before leaping into the surf.

$$$-$$ The Island Bali, 18 Gang Abdi, Jln Padma Utara, T0361 762722, www.the islandhotelbali.com. Bali's first true flash-packer venue blows the cobwebs of standard backpacker hostels with smart dorms, swish but small loft rooms, Wi-Fi access and even an infinity pool and cinema. Recommended.

$$$ All Seasons, Jln Padma Utara, T0361 767688, www.allseasonslegian.com. Top choice for mid-range travellers, with a slightly cramped but well-equipped hotel offering 113 rooms with pool facing views and cheery clean rooms with all mod cons. Breakfast and Wi-Fi are chargeable. For the

best rates, book online in advance.
Free shuttle service to Kuta offered.
Staff are excellent. Highly recommended.

$$$ Casa Padma Suites, Jln Padma,
T0361 753073, www.casapadmasuites.com.
Handy location for those keen to dive
straight into the drinking and shopping
action along Jln Padma, this hotel has large,
clean rooms with cable TV and chargeable
Wi-Fi access and slightly tatty furnishings.
The deluxe rooms are cavernous and would
suit a group travelling together. Bar, pool
and massage service.

$$$ The Lokha, Jln Padma Utara, T0361
767601, www.thelokhalegian.com. Well-run
hotel with 49 spacious, stylish rooms, some
with baths. 2 spacious pools, café, massage
service and Wi-Fi.

$$ Bali Sorgowi Hotel, Jln Legian, T0361
755266, www.balisorgowi.com. Down
a quiet alley on the Kuta/Legian border
this place is much touted on the internet,
comfortable pool-facing a/c rooms with
TV and fridge.

$$ Sinar Bali Jln Padma Utara, T0361
751404, www.hotelsinarbali.com. Tucked
away down an alley, this quiet hotel offers
clean, comfortable a/c rooms with TV and
bathroom. Good-sized pool. Recommended.

Seminyak *p28, map p29*

Long a favoured haunt of expats, some
of the accommodation in Seminyak is in
bungalows and houses available to rent
monthly or long term. Look for signs along
the streets, notices in the *Wartel* on Jln
Dhyanapura or the estate agents. For shorter
stays most places are in the mid- to upper
range with only a handful of budget options.
Those looking for a bit of rustic peace and
quiet away from the main drag should
wander along Jln Sarinande and Jln Saridewi
towards Jln Kayu Aya for a decent selection
of quiet, upmarket villas and guesthouses.

$$$$ Anantara, Jln Abimanyu, T0361
737773, www.bali.anantara.com. Hotel
offering unsurpassed views of the beach, the
59 gorgeous sea-view suites feature floor-to-

ceiling windows, terrazzo tub, iPod dock and
modern Balinese decor. 3 pools, including 1
infinity pool. 3 restaurants and a rooftop bar
with DJs spinning chill out tunes as the sun
sets. Free Wi-Fi access.

$$$$ The Elysian, Jln Saridewi 18, T0361
730999, www.theelysian.com. Beautiful
place with 26 1-bedroom villas and private
pool. Villas are ultra modern and come
with all the hi-tech goodies necessary for
computer addicts. Restaurant, massage
service and even an a/c library. Significant
discounts offered for online bookings.

$$$$ Le Jardin, Jln Sarinande 7, T0361
730165, www.lejardinvilla.com. A short stroll
from the beach, 11 2- to 3-bedroom walled
villas each with small private pool, dining
room, kitchenette and small garden. The
surrounding walls make each villa seem
slightly cramped. Well-furnished rooms
and friendly, professional staff. Facilities
include gym, health spa and Wi-Fi.

$$$$ Sun Island, Jln Raya Seminyak, T0361
733779, www.sunislandboutiquevillas.com.
22 spacious and stylish villas with private
walled garden. Each has private plunge pool,
kitchenette and bath tub. Private butler, chef
service and in-room spa treatments available.

$$$ Puri Cendana, Jln Camplung Tanduk
just off Jln Abimanyu, T0361 732947,
www.puricendanaresortbali.com.
Homely place a short stroll from the
beach offering comfortable and attractive
Balinese-style rooms with cable TV and
4-poster beds. Wi-Fi is available in the
lobby and around the pool.

$$$-$$ The Green Room, Jln Abimanyu
63B, T0361 731412, www.thegreenroombali.
com. Follow the signs down a small lane
off the main street. Sociable and popular
with young Europeans. De luxe a/c rooms,
simple fan rooms, pool, and a covered
decking area with plenty of cushions,
hammocks and Robinson Crusoe style.
Also has another relaxed place down
in Canggu. Recommended.

$$ Sarinande Beach Inn, Jln Sarinande 15,
T0361 730383, www.sarinandehotel.com.

Cheerful, with friendly staff. Spotless comfortable rooms with minibar, private terrace and private hot-water bathroom. Pool and restaurant serving Asian and Western cuisine. Reservations are necessary. Discounts available for stays of more than 14 days. Recommended.

Batubelig

$$$$ Balisani Suites, Jln Batubelig, Kerobokan, T0361 730550, www.bali-sani. com. 126 rooms and suites in peaceful seaside location. Built in Balinese village style, attractively decorated. Swimming pool, 4 restaurants and bars. Free shuttle to Kuta and airport transfers.

$$$ Batubelig Beach Bungalows, Jln Batubelig 228, Kerobokan, T0361 30078. Attractively furnished thatched roof bungalows, with kitchen, large bedroom and bathroom, hot water, a/c, set in garden. Peaceful location 3 mins' walk to the beach. Breakfast not included. Longstay rates available. **Sastika Restaurant** on premises, very cheap and good value.

$$$ Intan Bali Village, PO Box 1089, Batubelig beach, T0361 752191. A/c, several restaurants, 2 pools, extensive sports facilities, large central block with some bungalow accommodation. Caters almost exclusively to tour groups, with little to attract the independent traveller.

Canggu p28

The scenic countryside around Canggu is dotted with private villas, many of which are for rent. There are also many hotels being constructed and the sight of dumper trucks rattling along the rutted roads is common.

$$$ Hotel Pisang Mas, Jln Tibu Peneng, Jln Pantai Berawa, T0361 786 8349. Walled complex featuring 3 beautifully furnished 1-bedroom cottages built above a pool. There is a kitchen and outdoor dining area to seat 8. Would suit a group. Dogs barking incessantly outside are tiresome. The owner lives in Legian so needs to be contacted in advance.

$$$ Legong Keraton Beach Hotel, Jln Pantai Berawa, T0361 730280, www. legongkeratonhotel.com. Facing the sea, this spacious but somewhat characterless hotel has a/c rooms with TV and balcony. Sea-view rooms have bath. Hotel offers free daily shuttle service to Kuta. Restaurant, pool and open-air bistro serving Western food. Bike hire.

$$$ Villa Senyum, Jln Pemelisan Agung Jln Pantai Berewa, T0361 7464915, www.villa-senyum.com. Clean tasteful cottages with TV and attached bath with private balcony in an outstandingly peaceful location. Pool and restaurant.

Sanur p30, map p31

Accommodation on Sanur is largely mid-to high-range, though there are a couple of decent budget guesthouses along Jln Danau Tamblingan, which offer fair value for money. For the best rates, book high-end hotels well in advance. Walk-in rates can be astronomical. Unless otherwise stated, all accommodation includes private bathroom and Western toilet.

$$$$ Segara Village, Jln Segara Ayu, T0361 288407, www.segaravillage.com. Sprawling complex divided into 5 villages over the 5 ha, this place is popular with European and Australian tour groups and has simple, clean rooms, though lack the mod cons of other hotels in this price range. However, with good restaurant, 3 pools, tennis courts and weekly outdoors cinema there is no reason to spend too much time in the room.

$$$$ Tanjung Sari, Jln Danau Tamblingan 41, T0361 288441, www.tandjungsarihotel. com. 26 bungalows set in atmospheric grounds, each crafted in traditional Balinese style. Each bungalow is decorated differently and has different amenities – check first. Well-stocked library. Beachfront bar and restaurant. Recommended for a splurge.

$$$$ Villa Dampati, Jln Segara Ayu 8, T0361 288454, www.banyuning.com. 9 spacious 3-bedroom walled villas each with private garden and pool, internet access and a deep bathtub in immaculate bathroom.

$$$ Gazebo Cottages, Jln Danau Tamblingan 35, T0361 288212, www.baligazebo.com. 76 pleasant rooms in a range of styles. 3 smallish pools and large outdoor chess set, big, attractive Balinese-style gardens leading to the beach. Peaceful, friendly, reasonable value.

$$$ La Taverna, Jln Danau Tamblingan 29, PO Box 3040, T0361 288497, www.latavernahotel.com. Discounts available, restaurant (recommended), pool. 34 well-decorated rooms with safety box, attractive gardens leading down to the sea and not a particularly good beach. De luxe rooms have private pool and kitchenette. Broadband. *Legong* dance every Fri evening at 2030 in the restaurant.

$$$ Pondok Ayu, Jln Sekuta, Gang Pudak 3, T0361 284102, www.pondok.com.au. Australian-owned complex 15 mins' walk from the beach. There are 4 comfortable, homely rooms with TV and DVD player overlooking a small pool. The owner rents out her large suite when she is out of Bali. Free transport into town provided. Wi-Fi (chargeable) and decent breakfast provided. Good value. Book well in advance.

$$$ Scape Condotel, Jln Danau Tamblingan 80, T0361 281490, www.scapebali.com. Smart place just off the busy main drag with comfortable rooms facing a grassy garden and 22-m lap pool. Rooms feature a living room area with TV and DVD player. Free Wi-Fi throughout. Recommended.

$$$-$$ Swastika Bungalows, Jln Danau Tamblingan 128, T0361 288693, swastika@indosat.net.id. 81 rooms. Standard rooms have funky outdoor bathrooms and are cosy and filled with Balinese character. The de luxe a/c rooms are huge, but have a lot less character. 2 pools, quiet location set back from road, 15 mins' walk from the beach, pleasant gardens, popular with families, central for shops and restaurants.

$$-$ Little Pond Homestay, Jln Danau Tamblingan 19, T0361 289902, www.ellorabali.com. Undoubtedly the best budget bet in town with sparkling fan and a/c rooms facing a lap pool. The more expensive rooms have TV. The comfy fan rooms are great value. Free Wi-Fi. Recommended.

$ Yulia's 1 Jln Danau Tamblingan 38, T0361 288089. The owner's prize-winning songbirds fill the shady gardens with tropical banter in this friendly and popular place with spacious fan and a/c rooms. The spacious fan rooms with private balcony on the 2nd floor of the building at the back are great value.

🍴 Eating

Kuta *p26, map p27*

Most of the restaurants offer a range of food, including Indonesian and international cuisines. There is also a line of cheap *warungs* selling Indonesian favourites such as *nasi goreng* and *soto ayam* in the middle of Gang Ronta, joining Poppies 1 and 2.

$$$ Poppies, Poppies Gang 1, T0361 751059, www.poppiesbali.com. Open 0800-2300. In beautiful gardens, romantic **Poppies** is much favoured by couples. The menu offers a safe blend of good Indonesian and Western with dishes such as half-moon swordfish and delectable steaks. Serves famed Toraja coffee from Sulawesi. Reservations recommended.

$$ Kedai Tiga Nyonya, Jln Pantai Kuta 8-9, T0361 767218. Open 1000-2200. Delightfully furnished with gramophones and photos of the Straits Chinese community from the distant past, this top-rated eatery has a wide selection of Peranakan (Straits Chinese) fare with some Dutch flourishes (try the bitterballen). Juices are good and staff attentive. Recommended.

$$ Kopi Pot (and the Lone Palm Bar), Jln Legian, T0361 752614. Managed by the same people who run **Poppies**, the menu here skips gracefully from Sumatran fish curries and beef satay cooked table-side to greek salads and some delectable Indonesian coffees. The **Lone Palm Bar** is a good place to pull up a bar stool, sink a beer and catch up on some sporting action after dinner.

$$ Kori, Poppies Gang 2, T0361 758605, www.korirestaurant.co.id. Open 1200-2400. Soft jazz and tinkling water features provide mellow vibes. Indonesian and Western fare is washed down with 2-for-1 on selected cocktails most nights.

$$ Maccaroni, Jln Legian 52, T0361 754662, info@maccaroniclub.com. Open 0900-0200. Sleekly designed for the hipper tourist, diners eat fusion food and Western and Asian favourites to mellow pre-club beats.

$$ TJ's, Poppies Lane 1, T0361 751093. Open 0900-2330. Well-established and cheery Mexican eatery serving large portions of *fajitas* and *chimminchangas* with an extensive tequila cocktail list.

$$ Un's Paradise Restaurant, Un's Lane (off Jln Pantai Kuta), T0361 752607. Open 1700-2400. The tables in the peaceful courtyard are a fine spot to sample some Balinese dishes such as *gulai babi* (pork stew), Balinese-style *sate*, and seafood such as the excellent potato-wrapped red snapper fillet. Also serves fair Western cuisine. Excellent service.

$$-$ Made's Warung, Jln Pantai Kuta, T0361 755297, www.madeswarung.com. Open 0900-2400. A bit quieter than it used to be, this Kuta institution has a mind-bogglingly long and rambling menu of Western and Indonesian fare. Homely ambience with friendly service.

$ Warung 96, Jln Benesari (off Poppies Gang 2), T0361 750557. Open 1000-2400. Excellent pizzas served from a wood-fired oven are the highlight of this laid-back place popular with those fresh from the beach. Friendly service.

$ Warung Indonesia, Gang Ronta (off Poppies Gang 2), T0361 739817. Open 0900-2300. Menu of bog standard Indonesian favourites such as *nasi goreng* and *pecel lele*. The real highlight here is the extensive *nai campur* selection where you choose a selection of dishes to accompany your rice. Superb fresh fruit juices, laid-back vibes and cool reggae after the sun goes down, though the staff seem to become strangely spaced out as the moon rises higher in the sky.

Legian *p28, map p29*

Warungs are scattered along the beach selling simple local fare and drinks.

$$ Café Marzano, Jln Double Six, T0361 874 4438. Good value authentic Italian fare including pizza, salad, pastas and delectable tiramisu. They'll deliver to hotels for those feeling little worse for wear after a night on the Bintangs.

$$ Lanai, Jln Pantai Arjuna 10, T0361 731305. Open 0800-2300. Sea views and an eclectic menu that features sushi, sashimi and Mexican food. Decent kids' menu.

$$ Seaside, Jln Pantai Arjuna 14, T0361 737140, www.seasidebali.com. Open 1100-2300. Stunning sunset views at this cool beachside eatery dishing up international cuisine. Daily special offers. Popular for sunset drinks accompanied by chilled-out tunes.

$$-$ Wali Warung, Jln Padma Utara 16, T0819 3620 1874. Friendly and popular spot offering Western and Indonesian favourites. The real reason to come here is to sample the *babi guling* (roasted pig) or the seafood platter, both of which are huge and need to be ordered a day in advance.

$ Indonational, Jln Padma Utara 17, T0361 759883, www.indonationalrestaurant.com. Open 0900-2300. Popular Australian-owned restaurant that totes its high levels of hygiene. Rammed with Aussies most days chomping through their lengthy menu of Western and pseudo-Asian fare; family-friendly ambience.

$ Warung Yogya, Jln Padma Utara 79, T0361 750835. Open 1000-2200. Tasty Javanese dishes in a friendly setting. Popular with Dutch visitors. The hearty *nasi campur* and *soto rawon* are worth sampling. Recommended.

Seminyak *p28, map p29*

Food is taken seriously in this part of the world, and a diverse selection of excellent cuisine can be found here. Restaurants are concentrated along Jln Abimanyu, Jln Raya Seminyak and Jln Laksmana

$$$ Gado Gado, Jln Abimanyu, T0361 736966. Open 0800-2300. Located on the beach, this eatery is popular for sundown drinks and good international fare. Some superb seafood dishes. There is an extensive list of pasta dishes and salads. Good service.

$$$ Ku De Ta, Jln Laksmana 9, T0361 736969, www.kudeta.net. Open 0700-0200. Possibly the coolest dining venue in Bali with expansive views, gorgeous contemporary decor and superb selection of music including live performances. Menu features tasty, fresh and light fusion cuisine. Well worth a visit, even if just for a sunset cocktail.

$$ Pantarei, Jln Raya Seminyak 17 A, T0361 732567, adonis@indosat.net. Open 1100-0100. Delicious Greek staples such as *dolmades* and *bourek* in this friendly and well-lit restaurant popular with couples and families.

$$ Trattoria, Jln Laksmana T0361 737082. Open 1000-2400. Popular and friendly Italian restaurant with a menu that changes daily.

$$ Unico, Jln Kunti 7, T0361 735931. Superb value authentic Italian cuisine with very reasonably priced good-quality house wines, and an Italian owner who used to make more than 150 pizzas a day in Italy. Recommended.

$ Art Café, Jln Sari Dewi, T0361 737671. You can just about forget all about Kuta here in this quiet and open setting. The restaurant serves tasty sandwiches and healthy soups, has free Wi-Fi access and overlooks and calming lily-covered pond. The owner also has some good accommodation out the back (www.villakresna.com) for those who fall in love with the peace and quiet here.

$ Zula Vegetarian Paradise, Jln Abimanyu 5, T0361 731080. Serves up healthy treats such as pumpkin and ginger soup, amazingly wholesome falafel sandwiches and a range of zingy antioxidant drinks. Also a grocery attached that sells healthy products and has a noticeboard detailing local events. Recommended.

There is also a small family-run *warung* selling inexpensive grilled seafood on the beach in front of the **Dhyana Pura Hotel**.

Sanur *p30, map p31*

Sanur has a glut of eateries ranging from fine dining to cheap and cheerful backpacker cafés. The more expensive places are attached to the beachfront hotels. However, good food doesn't need to cost the earth and is readily available on the beach or along Jln Danau Tamblingan.

$$$ The Village Cucine Italiana, Jln Danau Temblingan 47, T0361 285025. Open 1100-2400. Italian food in a trendy lounge environment. The dishes are classic Italian and cover the range from meat, pasta and seafood. Good range of antipasti. Free unlimited broadband access.

$$-$ The Porch, Jln Danau Tamblingan 110, T0361 281682. Retro-styled place with friendly staff and long menu of Western treats like baked beans on toast and bangers and mash for homesick travellers. High tea, excellent sandwiches and extensive coffee menu keep this place busy. Free Wi-Fi. There's a small guesthouse out the back.

$$-$ Spikes Downtown Café, Jln Danau Tamblingan 174, T0361 28247. Unpretentious and friendly American diner themed eatery with extensive menu of burgers, Mexican favourites, milkshakes and apple pie with ice cream.

$$-$ Street Café, Jln Danau Tamblingan 21, T0361 289259. Open 0800-2300. Comfy and inviting café place with free book exchange, Wi-Fi, salad bar and menu of Turkish *pide* (similar to pizza), Balinese dishes and hearty breakfasts. Live music some nights.

$ Café Batujimbar, Jln Danau Tamblingan 75A, T0361 287374, www.cafebatujimbar. com. Open 0700-2230. Extremely popular, serving a crowd-pleasing mix of smoothies, toasted sandwiches and Indonesian favourites in a relaxed, modern setting. Recommended.

$ Manik Organik, Jln Danau Tamblingan 85, T0361 8553380. Australian-owned, this bright and cheery organic café sells a delicious range of healthy sandwiches, juices, curries and cakes (try the beetroot chocolate brownies) as well as organic beauty products. Nightly classes held in a room upstairs including belly dancing, meditation, yoga, tai chi and life drawing.

$ Rasa Senang, Jln Danau Tamblingan, T0361 289333. Promising Indonesian food with a Dutch touch, this friendly place offers a good selection of Indonesian and Balinese fare and 2 excellent value *rijstaffel* to choose from. The Indonesian burger served here is worth trying for its blend of flavours.

$ Smorga's, Jln Pantai Karang 2, T0361 289361. Open 0600-2100. Gourmet sandwiches with a range of fresh bread, coffees and gelato. Has the *Jakarta Post* to linger over. Good value and deservedly popular.

Sindhu Beach

There are plenty of places to choose from on Sindhu Beach.

$$-$ Beach Café, Sindhu Beach Walk, T0361 282875. Open 0900-2200. Good spot for a breakfast of eggs Benedict or even a full English with delightful views over to Nusa Penida. Good sandwiches, seafood and Mexican served throughout the day.

$$-$ Benno's, Sindhu Beach Walk, T0361 286638. Open 0700-2300. Long menu that is designed more to please a crowd of hungry Aussies rather than discerning gourmets. Good Aussie breakfast, Western favourites like chicken cordon bleu and some Indonesian favourites.

$$-$ Mango Beach, Sindhu Beach Walk, Open 0700-2300. Rasta-inspired place that offers live reggae after dark, and fair Western and Indonesian standards.

Cheap sunset beers and a simple menu of Indonesian dishes including excellent *ikan baker* (grilled fish) can be found at **Warunng Pantai Indah** (**$**) midway along the beach walk.

🎧 Bars and clubs

The Kuta to Seminyak belt has the most varied and certainly the wildest nightlife on Bali with venues for both the glamorous and the flip-flop crowd. Most of the bars are on Jln Legian. All these places are free for tourists, but locals often have to pay to enter. Generally speaking, as with hotels, the further north you are, the more glamorous the crowd.

Kuta *p26, map p27*

The Bounty, Jln Legian, T0361 752529. Open 2200-0600. Popular drinking hole akin to a UK highstreet club set on a recreated ship. Gets sweaty and raucous as the night progresses.

Eikon, Jln Legian 178, T0361 750701. Attracts a cool set of punters with DJs spinning varied tunes from house to hip hop. Happy hour 2100-2400. Well worth a visit.

Paddys, Jln Legian, T0361 758555, www.paddysclub.com. Open 1600-0300. Rebuilt after being destroyed in the 2002 bombings, and going from strength to strength. Plays commercial music much loved by the drunken hordes. 2-for-1 happy hour 1930-2300.

Sky Lounge, Jln Legian 61, T0361 755423. Open 24 hrs. Cocktails lovingly created at this popular spot, which is growing famous for its 14-day vodka-infused martini. Serves tapas during the day and early evening. Ladies drink for free 2200-2400 on Sun.

Vi Ai Pi, Jln Legian 88, T0361 750425. Tapas bar by day and transforming itself into a sleek lounge bar by night. This is not a bad place to get away from the beer swilling crowds for a touch of glamour in the heart of Kuta.

Legian *p28, map p29*

Cocoon, Jln Double Six 66, T0361 731266, www.cocoon-beach.com. More of a beach club than a nightclub, **Cocoon** occupies a prime sunset spot overlooking the beach and attracts well-known DJs to play chilled beats to a discerning audience. On Sun mornings it is transformed into a kids' club with clowns, breakfast menu and pool activities.

Dejavu, Jln Pantai Arjuna 7, T0361 732777.
Open 2100-0400. Stylish lounge bar with
gorgeous sunset views, popular with the
glamorous set. 2-for-1 happy hour 2100-2300.
Double Six Jln Arjuna, T0361 733067, www.
doublesixclub.com. Daily 2200-0600. Free
entrance Sun, Mon, Tue, 75,000Rp Wed, Thu,
Fri, Sat (includes 1 drink). Top international
and Indonesian DJs spin hard house at this
trendy venue that starts to fill up after 0200.
The Sandpit, Jln Pantai Double Six.
Beachside *warung* with good selection of
drinks. Perfect positioning for a sunset beer.

Seminyak *p28, map p29*
Bush Telegraph Pub, Jln Abimanyu, T0361
723963. Open 1100-0200. Serves icy Aussie
beers such as VB and Fosters and a range of
grub from Australian steak to Asian staples.
Q Bar, Jln Abimanyu, T0361 730923. Open
1800-late. Popular gay bar with a golden
stage area featuring live cabaret.

Sanur *p30, map p31*
Not known for its wild nightlife; evenings are
fairly sedate in Sanur. There are a few small
bars scattered along Jln Danau Toba that
could make for an amusing pub crawl.
Cat & Fiddle, Jln Cemara, T0361 282218.
Open 0730-0100. Live music, a good range of
booze and British food at this British-owned
pub popular with expats. Recommended.
Jimmy's Café, Jln Danau Toba. Popular
Aussie watering hole with thrice weekly
barbecues, cheap. Icy beer and sociable bar.
Lazer Sports Bar, Jln Danau Tamblingan
82, T0361 282840. Open 0900 until the last
customer staggers home. Keep up-to-date
with English football in this relaxed bar with
cold beers and live music on some nights.
Wicked Parrot, Jln Danau Tamblingan.

Entertainment

Kuta *p26, map p27*
Kecak, legong, Ramayana dance and Balinese
music; performances take place at many of
the major hotels.

Shopping

Kuta *p26, map p27*
Kuta is one of the best places on Bali to
shop for clothing; the quality is reasonable
and designs are close to the latest Western
fashions, with a strong Australian bias for
bright colours and bold designs. There is a
good range of children's clothes shops. Silver
jewellery is also a good buy (although some
of it is of inferior quality). Kuta also has a
vast selection of 'tourist' trinkets and curios.
Quality is poor to average. Almost all the
hawkers and stallholders are from Java.
They are unskilled workers who live in
cardboard boxes. This has led to a rise
in petty crime, and has sorely tried the
tolerance of the Balinese.

Batik PitheCanThropus, Jln Pantai Kuta,
T0361 761880. Open 0900-2230. Sells
everything and anything possible containing
elements of batik. Beautiful selection of
stock making this the ideal place to pick
up gifts to take back home.

Bookshops Periplus has a small but
decent selection of books on Bali and
Indonesia. Newspapers and the latest
bestsellers are also available here. There
is also a second-hand bookshop at the
beach end of Poppies Gang 2 selling
books in various languages.

Handicrafts Home Ide, Jln Legian,
T0361 760014, homeide2006@yahoo.com.
Open 0800-2300. Locally made accessories
for the home. Jonathan Gallery, Jln Legian
109, T0361 754209. Open 0800-2300. Well-
stocked with Balinese handicrafts including
wood carvings, jewellery and *ikat*. Uluwatu,
Jln Legian, T0361 751933, www.uluwatu.
co.id. Open 0800-2200. This local venture
sells handmade Balinese lace and elegant
white cotton clothing.

Shopping mall Matahari, T0361 757588.
Open 0930-2200. A popular alternative for

those fed up of haggling to pick up a wide selection of tourist trinkets at fixed prices.

Silver Ratna Silver, Jln Legian 72, T0361 750566. Open 0900-1000. Sells attractive contemporary silver jewellery made on Bali by a local artist. It has 3 branches on Bali. Other silver shops are along Jln Pantai Kuta and Jln Legian.

Supermarket In Matahari, selling fresh fruit and daily necessities.

Surfing clothes Surf Clothes Star Surf, Jln Legian, T0361 756251, open 0900-2230, and **Bali Barrel**, Jln Legian, T0361 767238, open 0900-2230, are both huge stores selling brand label surf wear at reasonable prices.

Legian *p28, map p29*
Hammocks Carga, Jln Padma Utara, T0361 765275. Open 0800-2200. Hammock specialist, friendly owner, expansive collection. Prices start at US$20 for a simple *ikat* hammock.

Handicrafts 'Antiques' and Indonesian fabrics at the north end of Jln Legian.

Swimwear and sportswear Several good shops on Jln Legian and side streets.

Seminyak *p28, map p29*
Jln Raya Seminyak is lined with interesting little boutiques, and shopping here is decidedly more upmarket than in Kuta. Locally made clothes and lifestyle stores dominate.
Clothes Neko, Jln Raya Seminyak, T0813 3738 7719, neko@telkom.net. Open 0900-2100. Cotton clothes made by 2 Balinese ladies. Welcoming staff and reasonable prices.
Paul Ropp, Jln Raya Seminyak, T0361 734 2089. Open 0900-2100. Bright cotton clothes made of fabric sourced in India and designed and made in Bali.

Sanur *p30, map p31*
Shopping in Sanur is a breeze if you've just arrived from the tout-ridden pavements of Kuta. There is the usual tourist stuff, including a beachside market along Sidhu beach selling cheap T-shirts, sunglasses and hats, but also some art shops and galleries to peruse.

Antiques Gotta Antique Collection, Jln Danau Tamblingan, T0361 292188. Open 0900-2200. Stocks a variety of antiques from around the archipelago, with a focus on carvings and *ikat* from eastern Indonesia.

Batik Puri Suar, Jln Danau Toba 9, T0361 285572. Open 0900-2000. Sells a colourful selection of locally made Balinese batik and *kebaya*.

Supermarkets Hardy's Supermarket, Jln Danau Tamblingan 136. Daily 0800-2230. Has a cheap supermarket, an optician's and a **Periplus** bookshop, stocking paperbacks, guidebooks, trashy magazines and postcards. **The Pantry**, Jln Danau Tamblingan 75, T0361 281008. Open 0900-2100. This grocery sells a range of Australian-produced goodies and has a good deli counter.

▲▲Activities and tours

Major hotels often have tour companies that organize the usual range of tours: for example, to Lake Bratan (where waterskiing can be arranged); to Karangasem and Tenganan to visit a traditional Aga village; to Ubud; whitewater rafting on the Agung River; to the temples of Tanah Lot and Mengwi; to the Bali Barat National Park; and to Besakih Temple.

Kuta *p26, map p27*
Body and soul
Numerous masseurs – with little professional training – roam the beach and hassle tourists on Jln Legian; more skilled masseurs can be found at hotels or specialist clinics around

Kuta. Jln Pantai Kuta has many aromatherapy and massage places.

Aroma Mimpi, Jln Pantai Kuta, Kuta Suci Arcade 12, T0361 762891. Open 0900-2400. Offers Balinese massage, body scrubs, facials and pedicures.

Dupa Spa, Jln Pantai Kuta 47, T0361 7953132. Open 0900-2400. 1-hr massage is 85,000Rp.

Diving

Aquamarine Diving, Jln Petitenget 2A, Kuta, T0361 738020, www.aqua marinediving.com. Owned and run by an Englishwoman, Annabel Thomas, a PADI instructor. It offers a personal service, uses Balinese Dive Masters who speak English (and Japanese) and has well-maintained equipment. PADI courses up to Dive Master can be provided in English, German, Spanish, French and Japanese. Dive safaris all over Bali and beyond are offered – check the website.

Surfing

Kuta is famous for its surfing, although the cognoscenti would now rather go elsewhere. Boards are available for rent on the beach at around 50,000Rp per hr. Bodyboards can be rented for 30,000Rp per hr. The guys renting boards on the beach offer surf lessons at US$15 for 2 hrs. Bargain hard.

Quicksilver Surf School, on the beach in Legian, www.quiksilversurfschoolbali.com. Offers more of the same at similar costs.

Rip Curl School of Surf, Jln Arjuna, T0361 735858, www.ripcurlschoolofsurf.com. This school has various packages. 30-min lesson US$65. Kids courses available starting at US$50.

Tubes, Poppies Gang 2, T0361 765726. Open 1000-0200. A popular meeting spot for surfers. The tide chart is posted outside and surfing trips to Java's **G-land**, www.g-land.com, can be boked here.

Tour operators

Amanda Tours, Jln Benesari 7, T0361 754090. One of the many tour operators offering full-day multi-stop tours to places

tuch as Kintamani, Tanah Lot and Lovina. Also offers car rental. Prices are negotiable.

Bali Adventure Tours, Jln Tunjung Mekar, T0361 721480, www.baliadventuretours. com. An organized company owned by long-term Australian resident, offers rafting or kayaking trips, mountain biking, elephant riding in Taro or trekking, US$23-89, including pick-up from hotel, lunch and insurance.

MBA, Poppies Gang 1, T0361 757349, www.mba-sensational.com. This company has branches all over Kuta, and offers domestic flight bookings, horse riding, river rafting and more.

Perama, Jln Legian 39, T0361 751875, www.peramatour.com. Organizes shuttle buses all over the island and tours further afield to destinations such as Flores and Lombok. **Perama** consistently manages to offer significantly cheaper fares than other operators and is developing something of a monopoly on the budget market. Gives a discount to passengers who present a used **Perama** ticket for travel on shuttle buses on Bali.

Water attractions

Head to Tuban, a 5-min taxi ride to the south of Kuta for the following:

Bali Slingshot, Jln Kartika Plaza, T0361 758838, www.balislingshot.net. Open 1100-late. US$25 (including T-shirt) per person. This Australian-owned ride involves being shot up into the air at ridiculous speeds, and advises tourists to 'make sure ya wear ya brown jocks'.

Waterbom Park, Jln Kartika Plaza, T0361 755676, www.waterbom.com. Daily 0900-1800. Adult US$26, child (under 12) US$16 (some rides and activities cost extra). Within walking distance of Tuban hotels, over 600 m of water slides in 3.8 ha of landscaped tropical gardens. Other facilities include water volleyball, spa offering traditional massage, etc, gardens, restaurant, lockers and towels for hire (children under 12 must be accompanied by an adult).

Legian *p28, map p29*
Bungee jumping
AJ Hackett at Double Six Club, Jln Arjuna,
T0361 752658, www.ajhackett.com/bali.
Mon-Fri 1200-2000, Sat and Sun 0029 until
0600. The 45-m leap of faith can be made
towering above the raving masses at this
popular nightspot. The price of US$99
includes a T-shirt, certificate and hotel pick-
up. For US$199, if you feel it is necessary,
you can be set on fire and then jump.

Diving and surfing
Scuba Duba Doo, Jln Legian 367, T0361
761798, www.divecenter bali.com. Dive
centre and school that runs 4-day Open
Water courses for US$375, and dive safaris
to various locations around Bali, including
Nusa Penida and Menjangan Island.
   Surfboards and bodyboards can be rented
on the beach for 50,000Rp and 30,000Rp
per hr, respectively.

Seminyak *p28, map p29*
Body and soul
Putri Bali, Jln Raya Seminyak 13, T0361
736852. Open 0900-2000. Javanese *mandi
lulur* scrub treatment where the body is
exfoliated using spices such as turmeric and
ginger and then bathed in a milk moisturiser.
Other local beauty treatments available here
include Balinese *boreh* wrap and a coconut
scrub technique imported from Sulawesi.
2-hr packages start at US$17.50.

Surfing
Surfboards and bodyboards are available
for rent on the beach. Bargain hard.

Canggu *p28*
Horse riding
Canggu Tua, T0361 747 0644. A 2-hr ride
including lunch costs US$50.
Tarukan Equestrian Centre, Jln Nelayan 29.

Sanur *p30, map p31*
Body and soul
Massages are also available at the beach.

Bali Usada Meditation Center, By Pass
NgurahRai 23, T0361 289209, www.bali
meditation.com. Courses in meditation.
Jamu Traditional Spa, Jln Danau Tamblingan
41, T0361 286595. Open 0900-2100.

Cruises
Bali Hai, Benoa Harbour, T0361 720331,
www.balihaicruises.com. Packages to Nusa
Lembongan from Benoa. Trips include the
Reef Cruise on the company's purpose-built
pontoon just off Lembongan. The *Aristocrat
Cruise* is on a luxury catamaran and includes
snorkelling, and use of the facilities at a
Lembongan beach club for the day (both
US$98 adult/US$66 child).

Dance
Tandjung Sari Hotel offers Balinese dance
lessons for children Fri and Sun 1500-1700.

Diving
Blue Season Bali, Jln Danau Tamblingan 69,
T0361 270852, www.baliocean.com.
A 5-star IDC centre offering PADI scuba-dive
courses, and a variety of other courses such
as Rescue Diver and Night Diver. Also offers
trips to Nusa Penida and Nusa Lembongan
and Tulamben .

Mountain biking
Sobek, Jln Tirta Ening 9, T0361 287059,
www.balisobek.com. Trips down the
mountainside from Gunung Batur to Ubud
with guide, buffet lunch and insurance;
US$79 adult, US$52 children (7-15).

Surfing
The reef here has one of the world's best
right-hand breaks, but it is only on for
about 28 days a year. It's best in the wet
season Oct-Apr, and is possible with any
tide depending on the size and direction
of the swell. Beware of strong currents and
riptides in high winds. To the north of Sanur,
the right-hand break in front of the **Grand
Bali Beach Hotel** is a fast 4-5 m with some
good barrels, but is best on a mid- or high-

tide and needs a large swell. Opposite the **Tanjung Sari Hotel** at high tide, there is the possibility of a long, fast wall. For the biggest waves, hire a jukung to take you out to the channel opposite the **Bali Hyatt**, very good right handers on an incoming tide.

Tour operators

Asian Trails, Jln By Pass Ngurah Rai 260, T0361 285771, www.asiantrails.info. Arranges hotels, flights and tours.
Nick Tours, Jln Danau Tamblingan (opposite Gazebo Hotel), T0361 287792, www.nick tours.com. Variety of tours offered from elephant trekking, swimming with dolphins and jeep safaris. Can help arrange visits to places outside Bali including to Komodo and Flores.
Perama, Warung Pojok, Jln Hang Tuah 39, T0361 287594. Island-wide shuttle bus.
Sobek, Jln Tirta Ening 9, T0361 287059, www.balisobek.com. Arranges birdwatching and sporting activities.

Watersports

Equipment is available from the bigger hotels or on the beach at Sindhu beach walk. Typical prices per person: jet ski US$25 per 15 mins; canoe US$5 per person per hr.
White Water Rafting Sobek, www.bali sobek.com, down Grade III rapids on Telaga Waju including professional guides, safety equipment and buffet lunch. US$79 adult, US$52 child (7-15).

⊖ Transport

Kuta *p26, map p27*

Kuta is the centre of **Perama** operations, Jln Legian 39, T0361 751551, in southern Bali and can arrange onwards transport to most Balinese destinations and beyond on their tourist shuttle buses. Prices include 4 daily connections to **Sanur** (US$2.50), 4 to **Ubud** (US$5), 1 to **Lovina** (US$12.50) and 3 to both **Candidasa** and **Padangbai** (US$6). They also go daily (1000) to the **Gili Islands** for US$35. A fast boat connection

from Serangan Harbour departs to **Nusa Lembongan** daily at 0630 (200,000Rp to Lembongan). **Blue Water Express** (T0361 895 1082, www.bluewater-express. com) departs daily for Nusa Lembongan (30 mins, 325,000Rp) and the **Gili Islands** (2 hrs, 690,000Rp) from Serangan Harbour. Free pick-up from hotels in southern Bali included in the price.

Legian *p28, map p29*
Car/motorbike hire

Sudarsana, Jln Padma Utara, T0361 755916. Open 0800-1800. Cars from US$16.50 per day (plus US$11 per day for a driver). Motorbikes US$5.50 per day.

Shuttle

To most tourist destinations on the island; shop around for best price. Perama is a good place to start. **Taxi** 40,000Rp to airport. The best metered taxi company is blue **Bali Taxi**, T0361 701111.

Canggu *p28*

To reach Canggu you will need your own transport. Follow the main road north from Legian until you pick up signs for Canggu. The beach signposted 'Canggu Beach' is in fact Pererean Beach. To reach Canggu Beach, turn left at the T-junction in Canggu village and keep going to the beach. The 25-min drive in a hired car should not cost more than 60,000Rp from the Kuta/Legian area.

Sanur *p30, map p31*
Air

Sumanindo Graha Wisata, Jln Danau Tamblingan, T0261 288570. Open 0800-1900. Domestic and international ticketing.

Bemo

Short hops within Sanur cost 5000Rp. There are connections on green bemos with **Denpasar**'s Kreneng terminal and on blue bemos with Tegal terminal (both 7000Rp).

Bicycle hire
25,000Rp a day.

Boat
Perama has a daily service to the surfer's and diver's mecca of **Nusa Lembongan** leaving at 1030 (1½ hrs) from the jetty at the north of town for US$12.50. Public boat leaves at 0800 and costs US$4. Ticket booth at beach end of Jln Hang Tuah. **Lembongan Fast Cruises**, Jln Hang Tuah, T0361 285522, www. scoot cruise.com. 4 sailings per day (0930, 1130, 1330, 1600), 30-min trip. US$50/US$30 for adult return/one way, US$43/25 child (13-16) return/one way and US$34/US$22 child (3-12) return/one way. Price includes pick-up and drop service. This company also offers daily connections to the Gili Island (Trawangan and Air) daily at 0930 via Nusa Lembongan (3 hrs, stopover at no extra cost permitted) US$125/US65 adult return/one way, US$85/US$45 child return/one way.

Car/motorbike hire
A1 Rental, (Jln Danau Toba, T0361 284287, offers cars at US$16.50 per day and motorbikes at US$6 per day.

Shuttles
Perama (see above) has 4 daily to **Ubud** (US$4), 5 daily to **Kuta** (US$2.50), and 3 daily to **Padangbai** (US$6).

Taxi
Most hotels will arrange airport transfer/pick-up and will charge the same, or more, than taxis (40,000Rp). A metered trip from one end of Sanur to the other is around 15,000Rp.

⊙ Directory

Kuta *p26, map p27*
Banks Bank Danamon, Jln Legian. Money changers on Jln Legian. Very few, if any, are licensed, and most are masters of sleight of hand and deception: take

a calculator with you and count your money *very* carefully. **Embassies and consulates** Netherlands, Jln Raya Kuta 127, T0361 751517, dutch consulate@ kcb-tours.com. Switzerland and Austria, Kompleks Istana Kuta Galleria, Blok Valet 2 No. 12, Jln Patih Jelantik, T0361 751735, swisscon@telkkom.net. **Internet** Turbo Internet on Gang Benesari and Top Sista on Gang Ronta offer fast connection. **Medical services** International SOS Bali, Jln Ngurah Rai By Pass, T0361 710505, sos.bali@internationalsos.com. Legian Clinic, Gang Benasari, T0361 758503. **Post office** Many; most open daily 0900-2000.

Legian *p28, map p29*
Banks Money can be changed in many places along Jln Padma Utara and Jln Legian. **Medical services** Padma Clinic, Jln Padma Utara 517, T0361 761484.

Seminyak *p28, map p29*
Banks Money changers and ATMs on Jl Raya Seminyak. **Internet** Jln Abimanyu. **Medical services** Pharmacy: Apotek Taiga Farma, Jln Raya Seminyak, T0361 730877, open daily 24 hrs. Clinic: Rahayu Clinic, Jln Adimanyu, T0361 774960. **Post office** Parking lot just off Jln Seminyak Raya.

Sanur *p30, map p31*
Banks Bank Mandiri, Jln Danau Tamblingan, 27. **Embassies and consulates** France, Jln Mertasari, Gang 2, No 8, Sanur, T0361 285485; Germany, Jln Pantai Karang 17, T0361 288535; Sweden and Finland, Segara Village Hotel, Jln Segara Ayu, T0361 288407; UK (also Ireland), Jln Tirta Nadi 20, T0361 270601. **Internet** Jln Danau Tamblingan and Jln Danau Toba. **Medical facilities** Dentist: Dr Alfiana Akinah, Jln Sri Kesari 17. Doctor: Bali Beach Hotel, daily 0800-1200. **Police** Jln Ngurah Rai, T0361 288597. **Post office** Jln Danau Buyan.

Ubud and around

Ubud is a rather dispersed community, spread over hills and valleys with deep forested ravines and terraced ricefields. For many tourists, Ubud has become the cultural heart of Bali, with its numerous artists' studios and galleries as well as a plentiful supply of shops selling clothes, jewellery and woodcarving. Unfortunately, the town has succumbed to tourism in the last few years, with a considerable amount of development.

During the rainy season Ubud gets more rain than the coastal resorts and can be very wet and much cooler.

Ins and outs → *Phone code: 0361.*

Getting there
Public bemos stop at the central market, at the point where Jalan Wanasa Wana (Monkey Forest Road) meets Jalan Raya, in the centre of Ubud. **Perama** ① *Jln Hanoman, T0361 96316,* which runs shuttle buses to the main tourist destinations, has a busy depot 15 minutes' walk away from the centre of town. Buses won't drop passengers off at accommodation. Arrivals are greeted with a small army of touts offering accommodation and transport. Public bemos run from Ubud to Batubalan for connections south including to Kuta and Sanur; Gianyar for connections east to Padangbai and Candi Dasa; and north to Singaraga and Louina and Kintaman. Perama also runs regular shuttles to the airport.

The **Bina Wisata tourist office** ① *Jln Raya Ubud (opposite the Puri Saren), open 0800-2000,* is good for information on daily performances and walks in the Ubud area, but otherwise not very helpful.

Sights → *For listings, see pages 51-56.*

Much of the charm and beauty of Ubud lies in the natural landscape. There are few official sights in the town itself – in contrast to the surrounding area (see page 48). The **Museum Puri Lukisan** ① *in the centre of Ubud, T0361 975136, www.mpl-ubud.com, 0900-1700, 40,000Rp,* contains examples of 20th-century Balinese painting and carving and that of Europeans who have lived here.

Antonio Blanco ① *T0361 975502, daily 0900-1800, 50,000Rp, walk west on the main road and over a ravine past Murnis Warung – the house is immediately on the left-hand side of the road at the end of the old suspension bridge,* is a Western artist who settled in Ubud has turned his home into a gallery. The house is in a stunning position, perched on the side of a hill, but the collection is disappointing. Blanco – unlike Spies and Bonnet – has had no influence on the style of local artists.

The **Museum Neka** ① *1.5 km from town, up the hill past Blanco's house, daily 0900-1700, 40,000Rp,* consists of six Balinese-style buildings each containing a good collection of traditional and contemporary Balinese and Javanese painting, as well as work by foreign artists who have lived in or visited Bali. There is a good art bookshop here and a good restaurant with views over the ravine.

ARMA (Agung Rai Museum of Art) ① *Jln Pengosekan, T0361 976659, www.arma museum.com, daily 0900-1800, 40,000Rp*, has a fascinating permanent exhibition of paintings by Balinese, Indonesian and foreign artists who spent time in Bali. It is the only place on Bali that exhibits the delightful work of Walter Spies, as well as famed Javenese artist Raden Saleh. Classical *kamasan* (paintings on tree bark) are displayed here, alongside works by the Balinese masters and temporary exhibitions featuring local photographers

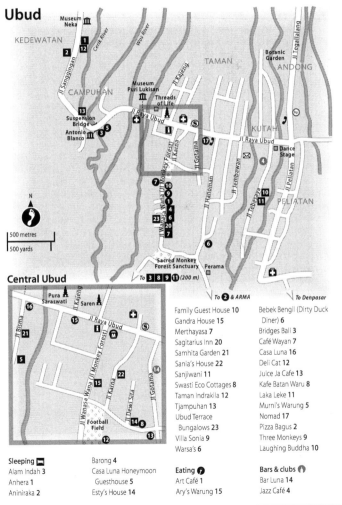

Ubud

Sleeping 🛏
Alam Indah **3**
Anhera **1**
Aniniraka **2**
Barong **4**
Casa Luna Honeymoon
  Guesthouse **5**
Esty's House **14**
Family Guest House **10**
Gandra House **15**
Merthayasa **7**
Sagitarius Inn **20**
Samhita Garden **21**
Sania's House **22**
Sanjiwani **11**
Swasti Eco Cottages **8**
Taman Indrakila **12**
Tjampuhan **13**
Ubud Terrace
  Bungalows **23**
Villa Sonia **9**
Warsa's **6**

Eating 🍴
Art Café **1**
Ary's Warung **15**
Bebek Bengil (Dirty Duck
  Diner) **6**
Bridges Bali **3**
Café Wayan **7**
Casa Luna **16**
Deli Cat **12**
Juice Ja Cafe **13**
Kafe Batan Waru **8**
Laka Leke **11**
Murni's Warung **5**
Nomad **17**
Pizza Bagus **2**
Three Monkeys **9**
Laughing Buddha **10**

Bars & clubs 🍸
Bar Luna **14**
Jazz Café **4**

and artists. The centre is also the venue for numerous cultural performances, and, more interestingly, for workshops on topics as diverse as Balinese dance, Hinduism in Bali, modernity in Bali and woodcarving. Recommended.

The **Bali Botanic Gardens** ① *Jln Kutuh Kaja, T0361 780 3904, www.botanicgardenbali. com, daily 0800-1800, 50,000Rp*, are 320-400 m above sea level and contain an impressive collection of ferns, palms, bamboo and other tropical trees. The garden is crisscrossed with pathways in a ravine. The garden also houses Bali's first maze, an Islamic garden and three teak *joglos* (Javanese traditional house) where simple food is served. **Threads of Life** ① *Jln Kajeng 24, T0361 972187, www.threadsoflife.com, daily 1000-1900*, a member of the Fairtrade Organisation, is a textile centre that provides an opportunity to learn about *ikat* and batik in Indonesia. There is a two-hour introduction course detailing the textiles and differences between hand-spun and commercial threads, essential if you are to purchase a pricey piece of *ikat*. The gallery has examples of *ikat* from Bali, Flores, Sumba, Sulawesi and Timor, showing the different regional motifs and contemporary uses. Talks on Tuesday (Introduction to Textiles of Indonesia – 150,000Rp for one to two people) and Wednesday (Textiles and their place in Indonesian Culture – 280,000Rp for one to four people). Register in advance.

At the south end of Jalan Monkey Forest is the **Sacred Monkey Forest Sanctuary** ① *daily 0830-1800, 20,000Rp, child 10,000Rp*, which is overrun with cheeky monkeys. An attractive walk through the forest leads to the **Pura Dalem Agung Padangtegal**, a Temple of the Dead. Back in town on Jalan Raya Ubud, opposite Jalan Monkey Forest, is the **Puri Saren**, with richly carved gateways and courtyards. West of here behind the Lotus Café is the **Pura Saraswati**, with a pretty rectangular pond in front of it. **Note** Do not enter the forest with food – these monkeys have been known to bite. You will only have 48 hours to get to Jakarta for a rabies injection.

The **Ubud Writers Festival**, www.ubudwritersfestival.com, held annually in October, attracts literary notables from Asia and beyond to participate in discussions on culture, society, politics and religion from a literary perspective. Workshops are held throughout the festival on travel writing, novel writing and short story writing. There are also cultural workshops held for those who wish to deepen their knowledge of all things Balinese.

Around Ubud

There are villages beyond Ubud that remain unspoilt and it is worth exploring the surrounding countryside, either on foot or by bicycle. Around Ubud, particularly to the north in the vicinity of Tampaksiring, and to the east near Pejeng and Gianyar, is perhaps the greatest concentration of temples in Bali. The most detailed and accurate guide to these *pura* is AJ Bernet Kempers's *Monumental Bali* (Periplus: Berkeley and Singapore, 1991). **Sangeh** and the **Pura Bukit Sari** are two temples about 25 km west of Ubud, but easier to reach via Mengwi.

Goa Gajah ① *15,000Rp, dress: sarong, a short ride by bemo from Ubud or from the Batubulan terminal outside Denpasar; alternatively, join a tour.* 'Elephant Cave', lies about 4 km east of Ubud, via Peliatan, on the right-hand side of the road and just before Bedulu. The caves are hard to miss as there is a large car park, with an imposing line of stall holders catering for the numerous coach trips. The complex is on the side of a hill overlooking the Petanu River, down a flight of steps. Hewn out of the rock, the entrance to the cave has been carved to resemble the mouth of a demon and is surrounded by additional carvings of animals, plants, rocks and monsters. The name of the complex is thought to have been given by the first visitors who mistakenly thought that the demon was an elephant. The small, dimly lit, T-shaped cave is man-made and is reached by a narrow passage whose entrance is the demon's mouth. It contains 15 niches carved out of the rock. Those on the main passageway are long enough to lead archaeologists to speculate that they were sleeping chambers. At the end of one of the arms of the 'T' is a four-armed statue of Ganesh, and on the other, a collection of *lingams*.

The **bathing pools** next to the caves are more interesting. These were discovered in the mid-1950s by the Dutch archaeologist JC Krijgsman, who excavated the area in front of the cave on information provided by local people. He found stone steps and eventually uncovered two bathing pools (probably one for men and the other for women). Stone carvings of the legs of three figures were uncovered in each of the two pools. These seemed to have been cut from the rock at the same time that the pools were dug. Water spouts from the urns, held by the nymphs, into the two pools.

Stairs lead down from the cave and pool area to some meditation niches, with two small statues of the Buddha in an attitude of meditation. The remains of an enormous relief were also found in 1931, depicting several stupas. To get there, walk down from the cave and bathing pools, through fields, and over a bridge. The complex is thought to date from the 11th century.

Yeh Pulu ① *350 m off the main Ubud–Gianyar road just south of the Tampaksiring turning, signposted to Bendung Bedaulu, bemos from Ubud will drop passengers at the turning; it is an easy walk from there to the site, dress: sarong and sash (for hire at site), it is probably possible to visit this site at any time, as there are no entrance gates, 60000Rp,* is 2 km east of Goa Gajah, beautifully set amongst terraced ricefields, and a short walk along a paved path from the end of the road. This is a peaceful place, free from crowds and hawkers. It is also the location of the local bath house. Yeh Pulu is one of the oldest holy places in Bali, dating from the 14th or 15th century. Cut into the rock are 20 m of vigorous carvings depicting village life, intermingled with Hindu and Balinese gods: figures carrying poles, men on horseback, Krishna saluting, wild animals and vegetation. Originally these would have been plastered over – and perhaps painted – although almost all of the plaster has since weathered away. A small cell cut into the rock at the south end of the reliefs is thought to have been the abode of a hermit – who probably helped to maintain the carvings. Until 1937 when the site was renovated, water from the overhanging paddy fields washed over the carvings causing significant erosion. There is also a small bathing pool here. An old lady looks after the small shrine to Ganesh and ensures a donation is placed there.

On the road north from Bedulu, Gianyar Regency contains a number of important archaeological sites, the majority located near **Pejeng**, 4 km east of Ubud. This sacred area, inhabited since the Bronze Age, contains over 40 temples as well as massive stone statues, carvings, sarcophagi, Buddhist sanctuaries, bathing sites and bronze artefacts. A number of artefacts have been removed to museums as far afield as Amsterdam, but many have remained *in situ*, beside rivers, in paddy fields or in nearby temples. Pejeng was once the centre of a great kingdom which flourished between the ninth and 14th centuries, before falling to the Majapahit. These days it is home to many Brahmin families.

The small, poorly labelled, **Purbakala Archaeological Museum**, consisting largely of a collection of sarcophagi, neolithic tools and Hindu relics, is 400 m north of Bedulu. About 200 m further north still is the **Pura Kebo Edan** ① *admission by donation, dress: sarong,* or 'Mad Bull Temple', a rather ramshackle and ill-kept temple. Among the monumental weathered stone figures in the courtyard is a statue of Bima dancing on a corpse, its eyes open, protected under a wooden pavilion. The figure – sometimes known as the 'Pejeng Giant' – is renowned for its 'miraculous' penis, pierced with a peg or pin (used to stimulate women during intercourse, a feature of sexual relations across the region).

Pura Pusering Jagat (the 'Navel of the World' Temple) is 50 m off the main road, a short distance north from Kebo Edan. **Pura Panataran Sasih** ① *admission by donation, dress: sarong, bemo from Ubud or from the Batubulan terminal outside Denpasar*, lies another 250 m north in Pejeng and is thought to date from the ninth or 10th century. This temple was the original navel *pura* of the old Pejeng Kingdom. The entrance is flanked by a pair of fine stone elephants. Walk through impressive split gates to see the '**Moon of Pejeng**' (*sasih* means 'moon'). It is housed in a raised pavilion towards the back of the compound and is supposedly the largest bronze kettledrum in the world. In Balinese folklore, the drum is supposed to have been one of the wheels of the chariot that carries the moon across the night sky. The wheel fell to earth and was kept (still glowing with an inner fire) in the temple. It is said that one night a man climbed into the tower and urinated on the drum, extinguishing its inner fire, and paid for the desecration with his life. Visitors should on no account try to climb the tower for a better look at the drum. The drum is believed to date from the third century BC, although no-one is absolutely sure – certainly, it has been housed here for centuries. It may be a Dongson drum from Vietnam or it may be a later example produced elsewhere. The fine decoration on this incomparable piece of bronze work was first recorded – in a series of brilliantly accurate drawings – by the artist WOJ Nieuwenkamp in 1906 (although it was mentioned in a book by the blind chronicler GE Rumphius, published in 1705). A collection of 11th-century stone carvings are also to be found here.

Gunung Kawi ① *6000Rp, dress: sash or sarong required, to get there catch a connection at Denpasar's Batubulan terminal or from Ubud to Tampaksiring, it is about a 3-km walk from here, passing Tirta Empul (see below), although bemos also make the journey to the temple site, the 'Mountain of the Poets'*, is one of the most impressive, and unusual, temples in Bali. A steep rock stairway with high sides leads down to the bottom of a humid, tree-filled, ravine. At the bottom lies the temple. The whole complex was literally hewn out of the rock during the 11th century, when it was thought to have been created as the burial temple for King Anak Wungsu and his wives, who probably threw themselves on his funeral pyre. You descend 315 steps to a massive rock archway, and from there to the nine tombs which face each other on either side of the Pakerisan River. These two rows of *candis*, four on the south side and five on the north, were cut out of the rock. It is believed that the five on the north bank of the river were for the king and his four wives, while the four on the south bank may have been for four concubines. They resemble temples and are the earliest traces of a style of architecture that became popular in Java in the following centuries. As such they may represent the precursor to the Balinese *meru*.

East of the five *candis*, on the far side of the river, is a cloister of various courtyards and rooms, also carved out of the rock. They were created for the Buddhist priests who lived here (visitors are asked to remove their shoes before entering). Still farther away, on the other side of the river, is the so-called 'tenth tomb'. The local people call this tomb 'The Priest's House'. The 10th tomb is, in all likelihood, a monastery and consists of a courtyard encircled by niches. To get to the 10th tomb take the path across the paddy fields, that runs from the rock-hewn gateway that leads down into the gorge; it is about a 1-km walk. There is accommodation close by in Tampaksiring, which also has a number of good jewellery workshops.

Tirta Empul ① *2 km north of Tampaksiring, 1 km on from Mount Kawi, 6000Rp, to get there take a bemo from Denpasar's Batubulan terminal or Ubud towards Tampaksiring, the temple is 2 km north of the town centre; either walk or catch a bemo, from here it is a 1-km walk to*

Gunung Kawi (see above), one of the holiest sights on Bali and is a popular pilgrimage stop, evident by the maze of trinket stalls. Tirta Empul is built on the site of a holy spring, which is said to have magical healing powers. In the past, *barong* masks were bathed here to infuse them with supernatural powers during the dance. Originally constructed in AD 960, during the reign of Raja Candra Bayasingha, the temple is divided into three courtyards and has been extensively restored with little of the original structure remaining – just a few stone fragments. The outer courtyard contains two long pools fed by around 30 water spouts, each of which has a particular function – for example, there is one for spiritual purification. The holy springs bubble up in the inner courtyard. During the **Galungan** festival, sacred *barong* dance masks are brought here to be bathed in holy water.

Ubud and around listings

For Sleeping and Eating price codes and other relevant information, see pages 7-10.

🛏 Sleeping

Ubud *p46, map p47*
Ubud has a great choice of good-value, clean and mostly high-quality accommodation, in often romantic and well-designed bungalows. Except in the more expensive hotels, breakfast is included in the rates. Cheaper accommodation often involves staying in a family compound providing a unique opportunity to watch the daily goings on of a Balinese family. Discounts of up to 30% available at expensive places in the low season. Book ahead in peak seasons. Those with a bit more cash to splash are advised to choose one of the places slightly outside town. These are generally far better value and often offer free shuttle service to and from town.

$$$$ Barong, Jln Monkey Forest, T0361 971758, www.barong-resort.com. A thatched reception filled with local antiques leads into a shady garden hosting 11 rooms. Tastefully decorated, in modern Balinese style, rooms have bathroom with sunken bath. De luxe rooms with private pool. Spa and 2 pools. Discounts available.

$$$ Casa Luna Honeymoon Gueshouse, Jln Bisma, T0361 977409, www.casaluna bali.com. Delightful selection of Balinese style rooms with 4-poster beds and spacious bathrooms and just on the edge of town. Good for a spot of romancing. Excellent breakfast included in the price. Recommended.

$$$ Samhita Garden, Jln Bisma, T0361 975443, www.samhitagarden.com. Far enough away from the town centre to escape the madness and calls for transport, yet close enough to be able to pop along to see a performance and have a decent meal every night, the **Samhita** offers spotless a/c rooms facing an inviting pool and well-tended garden. Spacious bathrooms.

$$ Sagitarius Inn, Jln Monkey Forest. The spacious open gardens are filled with an abundance of water features. Accommodation is in simple cottages with veranda. Pool.

$$-$ Merthayasa, Jln Monkey Forest, T0361 974176. Down towards the forest end of Jln Monkey Forest, this popular place has simple, functional clean fan rooms and some spacious comfortable a/c rooms, all facing a pool.

$$-$ Sania's House, Jln Karna 7, T0361 975535, sania_house@yahoo.com. Balinese cottages on a quiet street. A/c and fan rooms with comfy bed and clean bathroom. Popular.

$$-$ Ubud Terrace Bungalows, Jln Monkey Forest, T0361 975690, ubud_terrace@ yahoo.com. Situated in a quiet, verdant grove, a/c and fan rooms with attractive decor including Balinese-style 4-poster bed. Hot water, upstairs rooms have good sunset views. Pool. Recommended.

$ Esty's House, Jln Dewi Sita, T0361 980571. 6 well-maintained rooms with fan in quiet area, large and clean bathrooms. Recommended.

$ Gandra House, Jln Karna 8, T0361 976529. Good-value, simple clean fan rooms with veranda and hot water in friendly compound.

$ Warsa's, Jln Monkey Forest, T0361 971548, www.baliya.com/warsabungalow. Good location slap bang in the heart of the action, a/c and fan rooms here are very simple and cleanish. Bathrooms feature hot water, shower and *mandi*.

Nyuh Kuning Village

This small village just behind the Monkey Forest is home to ashrams, meditation centres and some excellent mid-range accommodation. Most places offer free shuttle service back and forth into town, or else it's a half an hour walk into the heart of town. There is a path skirting the Monkey Forest that is used by motorbikes and can be used by people staying at hotels in the village in order to avoid paying the forest admission fee everytime one wants to go home from town.

$$$ Alam Indah, T0361 974629, www. alamindahbali.com. This attractive and well-managed hotel offers Balinese-style rooms in verdant gardens, with some rooms offering stunning views over a riverine valley. Staff are friendly and great with kids making this an excellent choice for families. Excellent breakfast and afternoon tea, pool with attractive views and Wi-Fi access in some rooms. Recommended.

$$$ Swasti Cottages, T0361 974079, www.baliswasti.com. Peaceful place with organic garden producing some delcious veggies served in the restaurant, salt water pool and comfortable rooms. Very popular and well run. Recommended.

$$$ Villa Sonia, T0361 971307, www. soniahotel.com. Sonia's is a quiet spot offering comfortable accommodation in a variety of cottages set in a garden with a natural spring water pool.

West of Ubud Centre

The hotels to the west of Ubud offer breathtaking views and are often set among the rice paddies. However, they are a fair walk into town. Hotels are generally of high standard, and this is reflected in the prices.

$$$$ Anhera Jln Raya Sanggingan 168, T0361 977843, www.anherahotelbali.com. 8 rooms each designed to reflect one of the major Indonesian islands, some more tasteful than others. Spacious and comfortable rooms, with CD player and minibar. Obscenely large bathrooms feature jacuzzi with beautiful views of the rice terraces. 2 pools. Restaurant and spa facilities. Big discounts available.

$$$$-$$$ Tjampuhan, Jln Raya Campuhan, T0361 975368, www. tjampuhan-bali.com. Built in 1928 for the guests of the Royal Prince of Ubud, this charming hotel offers 67 well-decorated Balinese-style a/c and fan bungalows set on the side of a lush valley. The pool here is filled with spring water.

$$$ Aniniraka, Jln Raya Sanggingan, T0361 975213, www.aniniraka.com. 11 rooms surrounded by bright green rice paddies. Each of the large rooms has a kitchenette, dining area, spacious sleeping area and bathroom with sunken bath. Other facilities include a sauna and pool. 20% discounts available.

$$ Taman Indrakila, Jln Raya Sanggingan, T0361 975017, www.tamanindrakila.com. The view across the Sungai Cerik Valley is amazing, and is the main reason to stay here. 10 bungalows with Balinese-style 4-poster bed and balcony. Worn furniture, but reasonable value given the location. Wi-Fi access.

East of Ubud Centre

The streets lying to the east of the village centre are leafy and quiet, and are lined with Balinese family compounds. Jln Tebesaya and Jln Jembawan have a lot of good-value guesthouse accommodation.

$$ Family Guest House, Jln Tebesaya 39, T0361 974054, familyhouse@telkom.net. Spacious, well-decorated fan rooms with huge private balcony overlooking the forest, good value. Bath. Breakfast includes home-made brown bread.

$$ Sanjiwani, Jln Tebesaya 41, T0361 973205, www.sanjiwani.com. Clean fan rooms with hot water in a friendly and peaceful family compound. Residents can use the kitchen.

Eating

Ubud *p46, map p47*
Food in Ubud is good, particularly international. Most restaurants serve a mixture of Balinese, Indonesian and international dishes.

$$$ Ary's Warung, Jln Ubud Raya, T0361 975053. Open 0900-2400. Classy eatery serving up Asian and fusion cuisine and cocktails in a modern lounge-style setting. The *sake* and soya grilled salmon is worth investigating.

$$ Bebek Bengil (Dirty Duck Diner), Jln Hanoman, T0361 975489. Open 0900-2200. A renowned spot for Balinese duck dishes such as crispy fried duck, in a lovely setting that stretches out to the rice paddies behind. Popular.

$$ Bridges Bali, Jln Raya Campuhan, T0361 970095, www.bridgesbali.com. Located near the Blanco Museum, this smart place offers excellent contemporary fare, good wine selection and makes for a sound choice for those staying in this part of town.

$$ Café Wayan and Bakery, Jln Monkey Forest, T0361 975447. Open 0800-2300. Ubud favourite with its long menu of Balinese and international dishes and lip smacking cakes. The restaurant offers some garden seating. Head here on Sunday evenings for the Balinese buffet extravaganza with over 20 dishes to sample.

$$ Casa Luna, Jln Raya Ubud, T0361 977409, www.casalunabali.com. Open 0800-2300. Brunch here is scrumptious with a wide choice of Western favourites including a superb eggs Benedict. Throughout the day the kitchen produces excellent Balinese and Mediterranean fare in an elegant breezy setting with a green paddyfield view. Highly recommended.

$$ Kafe Batan Waru, Jln Dewi Sita, T0361 977528. Attractive eatery with colonial-era botanical drawings and old Indonesian city maps covering the walls. The food is excellent and this place offers possibly the best place in Ubud to try regional Indonesian cuisines such as *ayam rica rica* (from Sulawesi), *sayur belado* (from Sumatra) and *ayam taliwang* (Bali). Sun night is satay festival night with variety of satay to try. Good cocktail menu. Highly recommended.

$$ Laka Leke, Nyuh Kuning Village, T0361 977565, www.lakaleke.com. Fair international and Indonesian fare here, with excellent service on the edge of the rice paddies which are delightfully illuminated by lanterns after sunset. The real reason to come here is to see the dance performances (4 nights a week). Check the website for schedule.

$$ Laughing Buddha, Jln Monkey Forest, T0361 970928. Open 0900-0000. Small but attractive place offering contemporary Asian dishes, tapas and some Mediterranean fare and good range of devilish cocktails to accompany their live music evenings on Mon, Thu and Sat. Free Wi-Fi. 2-for-1 happy hour 1600-1900.

$$ Murni's Warung, Jln Raya Campuhan, T0361 975233, www.murnis.com. Open 0900-2100. Long menu of Western and Indonesian dishes. The Balinese food is worth trying, particularly the *betutu ayam* (chicken slow cooked in local spices for 8 hrs).

$ Art Kafe, Jln Monkey Forest, T0361 970910. Homely spot with pastel walls, scatter cushions, book and excange and free Wi-Fi, this is a pleasant spot to pass and hour or 2. Menu features Indonesian and Balinese dishes, though the owner claims the real crowd pleasers are the Mexican items. Live music 3 nights a week.

$ Deli Cat, Jln Monkey Forest, by the football pitch, T0361 971284. Open 0900-2400. Very good value, proffers tasty sausages and cheeses from around the world, chunky sandwiches, and hearty fish and meat main courses. The owner, from Iceland, has set the place up with sociable long benches, so expect interesting conversation while you get stuck into your bratwurst. Recommended.

$ Juice Ja Café, Jln Dewi Sita, T0361 971056. Open 0730-2200. Laid-back organic café serving good range of fruit juices, salads and tasty bagels with delightful toppings such as kalamata olive cream cheese. The health cocktails here are very popular. There is also a noticeboard detailing interesting local events.

$ Nomad, Jln Ubud Raya 35, T0361 977169, www.nomad-bali.com. Open 0900-2200. Popular for its fantastic selection of fresh pasta dishes, soups, juices and salads. Good range of teas from around the world. Nice upbeat atmosphere.

$ Pizza Bagus, Jln Pengosekan, T0361 978520, www.pizzabagus.com. Open 0830-2230. Popular Italian place serving the best pizza in Ubud, along with fine pasta and salads. There is a deli attached that makes sandwiches and sells cheeses, hams and German chocolate biscuits. The weekly organic farmers market is held here on Sat 0930-1400. Recommended.

$ Three Monkeys, Jln Monkey Forest, T0361 974830. Open 0700-2300. Popular place with a great menu of fresh pastas, salads and some scrumptious and unorthodox desserts. Also Javanese chocolate bars on sale. The breezy rice field out the back is a big plus.

🎵 Bars and clubs

Ubud *p46, map p47*
Ubud isn't exactly a centre of hedonism and most places shut around 0100. However, there are a few spots for an evening drink. **Bar Luna**, Jln Goutama, T0361 971832. Open 0800-2300. Relaxed and friendly spot claiming to be the home of the town's intellectual elite. Thu night is Literary Night and offers the chance for a bit of lively banter. **Jazz Café**, Jln Sukma, T0361 976594, www.jazzcafebali.com. Open Tue-Sun until 0100. Atmospheric surroundings make this a relaxed place for a drink or meal (cheap), with enticing menu and good live music. Free pick up service from **Laughing Buddha Bar** or hotels around Ubud offered.

🎭 Entertainment

Ubud *p46, map p47*
Art
Ubud has perhaps the greatest concentration of artists in Indonesia, exceeding even Yogya. Many will allow visitors to watch them at work in the hope that they will then buy their work. The **Pengosekan Community of Artists** is on Jln Bima.

Dance and cultural performances
Ubud has the most accessible cultural performances in Bali, with nightly events at various locations scattered around town, and in villages around Ubud. Transport is usually included in the cost of the ticket if the venue is outside Ubud. Performances start around 1930 and last for 2 hrs, but this varies so check beforehand. Tickets cost between US$5 and US$16.50 and are available from Ubud Tourist Information on Jln Ubud Raya, or at the venue. Go to the tourist office to check performance and venue. Recommended dances are the legong dance, the barong dance and the *kecak* dance. The **Puri Saren** on Jln Raya Ubud is a convenient and charming venue.

Ubud *p46, map p47*

Art Ubud painters have a distinctive style, using bright colours and the depiction of natural and village scenes. There is a large selection of paintings in the town and galleries are concentrated along the east section of Jln Raya Ubud. It is possible to visit the artists in their homes; enquire at the galleries. **Macan Tidur**, Jln Monkey Forest, T0361 977121, www.macan-tidur-textiles.com. Excellent selection of stylishly presented ethnographica. **Nikini Art**, Jln Monkey Forest, T0361 973354. Open 0800-2200. Has a fascinating range of *ikat*, carvings and silver from Timor. **Tegun Folk Art Galeri**, Jln Hanoman 44, T0361 970581. Daily 0800-2100. The overwhelming collection of eye-catching art and crafts from across the archipelago is well worth a browse. The owner is very friendly and has excellent English.

Bookshops Ganesha Bookshop, Jln Raya Ubud, T0361 970320. Fair selection of new and second-hand tomes, some maps, postcards and stationery. Periplus, Jln Monkey Forest. Open 0900-2200. Postcards, newspapers and a good selection of Indonesia-related books.

Textiles Kuno Kuno Textile Gallery, Jln Monkey Forest, T0361 973239. Open 1000-1900. Has decent quality *ikat* and batik.

Woodcarving Concentrated on the Peliatan road out of town. The so-called 'duck man' of Ubud (Ngurah Umum) is to be found on the road to Goa Gajah, with a selection of wooden fruits and birds. Recommended shop near the **Bamboo Restaurant**, off Jln Monkey Forest, facing the football field.

Ubud *p46, map p47*

Ubud has turned into something of an 'alternative' centre, and there is plenty to do here. Many people come to learn something, while others enjoy pottering about the countryside on 2 wheels.

Body and soul

Iman Spa, Jln Sri Wedari 8, T0812 3600 9610, www.imanspa.com. Open 1000-2100. Treatments include Balinese *boreh* and Javanese *mandi lulur*. Packages start at US$12. **The Yoga Barn**, Jln Pengosekan, T0361 970992, www.theyogabarn.com. Classes start at US$10. This well-regarded centre offers an assortment of yoga, meditation and t'ai chi classes daily, in a relaxed and green setting at the edge of town.

Birdwatching

The **Bali Bird Club**, www.balibirdwalk.com, sets off on walks around the Ubud countryside, on trails that differ according to the season. Birds that can be spotted include the Java kingfisher, bar-winged prinia, the black-winged starling and other birds endemic to Indonesia. The sociable 3½-hr walks leave from the **Beggar's Bush Pub** at 0900 on Tue, Fri, Sat and Sun. The price of US$37 includes lunch and water along the trail. Other rambles can be organized in demand; check the website.

Bike tours

Bali Eco, T0361 975557, www.balieco cycling.com. Small-group tours which start with breakfast overlooking Gunung Batur and then cruise downhill through villages to Ubud for 2½ hrs. Includes a walk around a coffee plantation, visit to a temple and decent Balinese buffet lunch in a family compound. US$36 per person (US$25 for children under 12), including hotel pick-up and drop off. Recommended.

Cooking

Casa Luna Cooking School, Jln Bisma, T0361 977409, www.casalunabali.com. Run by the owner of **Casa Luna** restaurant Janet de Neefe, this school offers the chance to explore the spices and kitchen myths of Bali. Each lesson concludes with a Balinese meal and cooking notes to take home. Different menu each day. Each lesson is around 4 hrs. US$30 per person. Recommended.

Ibu Wayan Cooking Classesl, T0361 975447. Ibu Wayan and her daughter Wayan Metri provide Balinese cooking classes for groups and have a list of the food to be learned each day. The 2-hr lessons are followed by lunch or dinner. Morning or afternoon lessons US$35 per person. Phone ahead to reserve. Small groups. Classes held at **Laka Leke** restaurant in Nyuh Kuning village.

Nomad's Organic Farm. Owner Nyoman throws open the gates of his organic farm in the village on Baturiti on Sun and Wed for an explanation of the different methods of organic farming and a lunch of salad made from vegetables chosen by the visitors. Enquire at **Nomad** restaurant (see Eating).

Tour operators

Perama, Jln Hanoman, T0361 973316.

⊖ Transport

Ubud *p46, map p47*
Bemo

These leave from the Pasar Ubud in the centre of town, at the junction of Jln Monkey Forest and Jln Raya Ubud; regular connections with **Denpasar**'s Batubulan terminal (Brown – 8000Rp), Gianyar (Green – 8000Rp). **Perama** has 5 daily departures to **Kuta**/airport (US$5), 5 departures to **Sanur** (US$4), 1 daily to **Lovina** (US$12.50), 3 departures to **Padangbai** (US$5) and 1 daily further afield to **Senggigi** from (US$15) and the **Gili Islands** (US$35). A ride to the airport or Kuta in a taxi costs arounds US$20.

Bicycle hire

Bicycles are the best way to get about (apart from walking); there are several hire places on Jln Monkey Forest, US$2.50 per day.

Car hire

Hire shops on Jln Monkey Forest, US$15 per day plus insurance for Suzuki 'jeep'; US$20 per day for larger Toyota Kijang.

Motorbike hire

Several outfits on Jln Monkey Forest, from US$7 per day.

❶ Directory

Ubud *p46, map p47*

Banks Numerous money changers will change cash and TCs and offer rates similar to banks. **Internet** Jln Monkey Forest. **Medical services** Clinic: Taruna Medical Centre, Jln Monkey Forest, T0361 781 1818, 24 hrs. Pharmacy: Apotek Mertasari, Jln Monkey Forest, T0361 972351, 0900-2130. **Police** Jln Andong, T0361 975316. **Post office** Jln Jembawan 1 (road running south off Jln Raya Ubud, opposite Neka Gallery) daily 0800-1800, poste restante.

Gianyar to Gunung Batur via Bangli

East of Ubud is the royal town of Gianyar. Some 15 km north of Gianyar, at the foot of Gunung Batur, is another former royal capital, Bangli, with its impressive Kehen Temple. A further 20 km leads up the slopes of Gunung Batur to the crater's edge – one of the most popular excursions in Bali. Along the rim of the caldera are the mountain towns of Penelokan and Kintamani, and the important temples of Batur and Tegen Koripan. From Penelokan, a road winds down into the caldera and along the west edge of Danau Batur. It is possible to trek from here up the active cone of Gunung Batur (1710 m), which thrusts up through a barren landscape of lava flows. North from Penulisan, the road twists and turns for 36 km down the north slopes of the volcano, reaching the narrow coastal strip at the town of Kubutambahan.

Gianyar → *For listings, see pages 62-64. Phone code: 0361.*

Gianyar is the former capital of the kingdom of Gianyar and in the centre, on Jalan Ngurah Rai, is the **Agung Gianyar Palace**, surrounded by attractive red-brick walls. At the turn of the century, the Regency of Gianyar formed an alliance with the Dutch in order to protect itself from its warring neighbours. As a result, the royal palace was spared the ravages and destruction, culminating in *puputan*, that befell other royal palaces in South Bali during the Dutch invasion. The rulers of Gianyar were allowed a far greater degree of autonomy than other Rajas; this allowed them to consolidate their wealth and importance, resulting in the regency's current prosperity and the preservation of the royal palace. It is not normally open to the public but the owner, Ide Anak Agung Gede Agung, a former politician and the Raja of Gianyar, does let visitors look around his house if you ask him. The bemo station is five minutes' walk to the west of the palace, also on Jalan Ngurah Rai.

Traditionally regarded as Bali's weaving centre, there is only a limited amount of cloth on sale these days. There is accommodation at **Agung Gianyar Palace Guesthouse ($$$)**, within the palace walls.

Bangli → *For listings, see pages 62-64. Phone code: 0366.*

Bangli, the former capital of a mountain principality, is a peaceful, rather beautiful town, well maintained and spread out. Set in a rich farming area in the hills, there is much to enjoy about the surrounding scenery, especially the captivating views of the volcanic area to the north including Gunung Agung and Gunung Batur. Both the town itself and the countryside around afford many opportunities for pleasant walks. The area claims to have the best climate on Bali and the air is cooler than on the coast. Despite these attractions, Bangli is not on the main tourist routes and is all the more charming for that.

Tourist information

The **Bangli Government Tourism Office** ① *Jln Brigjen Ngurah Rai 24, T0366 91537, Mon-Sat 0700-1400*, is very friendly and helpful, but little English is spoken and they are not really geared up for foreigners. A free booklet and map are available.

Background

Balinese believe that Bangli is the haunt of *leyaks* (witches who practise black magic). In Bali, misfortune or illness is frequently attributed to *leyaks*, who often intervene on behalf of an enemy. In order to overcome this the Balinese visit a *balian* (a shaman or healer), who often has knowledge of the occult. As a result of the presence of *leyak* in the area, Bangli has a reputation for the quality of its *balian*, with supplicants arriving from all over the island, dressed in their ceremonial dress and bearing elaborate offerings. The people of Bangli are also the butt of jokes throughout Bali, as Bangli is the site of the island's only mental hospital, built by the Dutch.

Sights

There is a **market** every three days in the centre of town. Locally grown crops include cloves, coffee, tobacco, vanilla, citrus fruit, rice, cabbages, corn and sweet potatoes; some of which are exported. Bangli lies close to the dividing line between wet-rice and dry-rice cultivation.

Most people come to Bangli to visit the **Pura Kehen** ① *6000Rp per person for a car, on the back road to Besakih and Penelokan, outside there are stalls selling snacks and sarongs*, one of Bali's more impressive temples and one of the most beautiful, set on a wooded hillside about 2 km to the north of the town centre. The *pura* was probably founded in the 13th century. There is some dispute over the true origin of the temple, because inscriptions within the compound have been dated to the ninth century. It is the second largest on Bali and the state temple of Bangli regency. Elephants flank the imposing entrance, leading up to three terraced courtyards, through finely carved and ornamented gateways decorated with myriad demons. The lower courtyard is dominated by a wonderful 400-year-old *waringin* tree (*Ficus benjamina*), with a monk's cell built high up in the branches. It is here that performances are held to honour the gods. The middle courtyard houses the offertory shrines, while the top courtyard contains an 11-tiered *meru* with a carved wood and stone base. The elaborate woodwork here is being beautifully restored and repainted by craftsmen. In the wall below, guides will point out the old Chinese plates cemented into it. Curiously, some of these depict rural England, with a watermill and mail coach drawn by four horses. Every three years in November (Rabu Kliwon Shinta in the Balinese calendar), at the time of the full moon (*purnama*), a major ceremony, **Ngusabha**, is held at the temple.

The **Sasana Budaya Arts Centre** stages performances of traditional and modern drama, music and dance, as well as art and cultural exhibitions. It is one of the largest cultural centres on Bali, located about 100 m from the Pura Kehen. Ask at the tourist office for information on performances. Bangli is particularly noted for its dance performances. Bangli also has one of the largest *gamelan* orchestras on Bali, captured from the ruler of Semarapura by the Dutch, who gave it to Bangli.

In the centre of town is the **royal palace**, which houses eight branches of the former royal family. Built about 150 years ago and largely restored by the present descendants, the most important section is the Puri Denpasar where the last ruler of Bangli lived until his death almost 40 years ago. The temple of the royal ancestors is situated on the northwest side, diagonally opposite the **Artha Sastra Inn**; important ceremonies are still held here.

There is an impressive **Bale Kulkul** in the centre of town, three storeys high and supported on columns made of coconut palm wood; it is about 100 years old. There are in fact two *kulkul, kulkul lanang* which is male, and *kulkul wadon* which is female. In times past the *kulkul* was sounded to summon the people, or act as an alarm warning of impending danger. The people of Bangli consider these *kulkul* to be sacred, and they are used during important temple festivals.

At the other end of town, the **Pura Dalem Penjungekan** (Temple of the Dead) is also worth a visit. The stone reliefs vividly depict the fate of sinners as they suffer in hell; hanging suspended with flames licking at their feet, being castrated, at the mercy of knife-wielding demons, being impaled or having their heads split open. The carvings are based on the story of Bima on his journey to rescue the souls of his parents from hell. The destructive 'Rangda' features extensively. In the centre there is a new shrine depicting tales of Siwa, Durga and Ganesh. The temple is in a parkland setting with possibilities for walks.

Around Bangli

There are a number of pleasant places to visit, including **Bukit Demulih** ① *walk or take a bemo bound for Tampaksiring, get off after about 3 km, take the narrow, paved road south for 1 km to Demulih village*, at an altitude of about 300 m. This small, pretty village has some well-carved temples, and a *kulkul* tower by the *bale banjar*. From here the villagers will show you the track up the hill, at the top of which is a small temple; on the way you pass a sacred waterfall. If you walk along the ridge you will come to other temples and fine views over the whole of South Bali.

A pleasant walk east of Bangli leads to **Sibembunut**. **Bukit Jati**, near Guliang about 2 km south of Bunutin, is another hill to climb for splendid views and scenic walks.

Sidan, just north of the main Gianyar–Semarapura road, 10 km south of Bangli, is notable for its **Pura Dalem** ① *6000Rp, car park opposite the temple, and a stage where dance performances sometimes take place*, which has some of the most vivid, spine-chilling depictions of the torture and punishment that awaits wrong-doers in hell. The carvings show people having their heads squashed, boiled or merely chopped off, and the wicked and evil widow Rangda dismembering and squashing babies.

Gunung Batur → *For listings, see pages 62-64.*

The spectacular landscape of Gunung Batur is one of the most visited inland areas on Bali. Despite the hawkers, bustle and general commercialization, it still makes a worthwhile trip. The huge crater – 20 km in diameter – contains within it **Danau Batur** and the active **Gunung Batur** (1710 m), with buckled lava flows on its slopes. The view at dawn from the summit is stunning. Although these days Gunung Batur is less destructive than Gunung Agung, it is the most active volcano on Bali having erupted 20 times during the past 200 years. Danau Batur in the centre of the caldera is considered sacred.

Trekking

A steep road winds down the crater side, and then through the lava boulders and along the west shore of Danau Batur. There are hot springs here and paths up the sides of Gunung Batur, through the area's extraordinary landscape. Treks begin either from **Purajati** or **Toya Bungkah** (there are four-, five- or six-hour treks), or around the lake (guides are available from **Lake View Cottages** in Toya Bungkah). Aim to leave Toya Bungkah at about 0330. After reaching the summit it is possible to hike westwards along the caldera rim, though

The Bali Aga: the original Balinese

In pre-history, Bali was populated by animists whose descendants today are represented by the Bali Aga, 'Original Balinese'. The Aga are now restricted to a few relic communities in North and East Bali, particularly in the regency of Karangkasem. Most have been extensively assimilated into the Hindu-Balinese mainstream. Miguel Covarrubias visited the Aga village of Tenganan in the 1930s, a village which even then was extraordinary in the extent to which it was resisting the pressures of change. He wrote:

"The people of Tenganan are tall, slender and aristocratic in a rather ghostly, decadent way, with light skins and refined manners ... They are proud and look down even on the Hindu-Balinese nobility, who respect them and leave them alone. They live in a strange communistic ... system in which individual ownership of property is not recognized and in which even the plans and measurements of the houses are set and alike for everybody."

Even today, a distinction is still made between the Bali Aga and the Wong Majapahit. The latter arrived from Java following the fall of the Majapahit Kingdom at the end of the 15th century.

In former years, the Aga were probably cannibalistic. It has been said that Aga corpses used to be washed with water, which was allowed to drip onto a bundle of unhusked rice. This was then dried and threshed, cooked, moulded into the shape of a human being, and served to the relatives of the deceased. The eating of the rice figure is said to symbolize the ritual eating of the corpse, so imbibing its powers.

---

this hike is not for the faint-hearted as the ridge is extremely narrow in places with steep drops on both sides. The cinder track passes several of the most active craters, lava flows and fumaroles. In the north and east of the caldera the landscape is quite different. The rich volcanic soil, undisturbed by recent lava flows, supports productive agriculture. The vulcanology institute on the rim of the caldera monitors daily seismic activity.

Trunyan

Boats can be hired from the village of **Kedisan** on the south shore of Danau Batur (be prepared for the unpleasant, hard-line sales people here) or from Toya Bungkah, to visit the traditional Bali Aga village (see box, above) of Trunyan and its cemetery close by at **Kuban**, on the east side of the lake.

The Bali Aga are the original inhabitants of Bali, pre-dating the arrival of the Majapahit; records show that the area has been inhabited since at least the eighth century. Trunyan's customs are different from Tenganan – but these differences can only be noted during festival time, which tend to be rather closed affairs. Despite its beautiful setting beside Danau Batur with Mount Abang rising dramatically in the background, a visit can be disappointing. Most people come to visit the cemetery to view the traditional way of disposing of corpses. Like the Parsees of India, corpses are left out to rot and be eaten by birds rather than being buried or cremated. It is claimed that the smell of rotting corpses is dissipated by the fragrance of the sacred banyan tree. The idea behind this custom is that the souls of the dead are carried up towards heaven by the birds; this flight to heaven propitiates the gods and results in improved prospects for the souls in their reincarnation in the next life. The corpses are laid out on enclosed bamboo rafts, but very likely all you will see is bones and skulls. The cemetery is only accessible by boat; make sure you pay at the end of your journey, otherwise the boatman may demand extra money for the return journey. The villagers are unfriendly and among the most aggressive on Bali; with a long tradition of begging for rice from other parts of the island as they were unable to grow their own. They now beg or demand money from tourists.

Penelokan and Kintamani
On the west rim of the crater are two villages, Penelokan and Kintamani. Large-scale restaurants here cater for the tour group hordes. The area is also overrun with hawkers selling batik and woodcarvings.

Penelokan is perched on the edge of the crater and its name means 'place to look'. About 5 km north of here, following the crater rim, is the rather drab town of **Kintamani**, which is a centre of orange and passionfruit cultivation. The town's superb position overlooking the crater makes up for its drabness. Ask locally for advice on the best walks in the area and for a guide for the more dangerous routes up to the crater rim.

Pura Batur
Just south of Kintamani is Pura Batur, spectacularly positioned on the side of the crater. This is the new temple built as a replacement for the original Pura Batur, which was engulfed by lava in 1926. Although the temple is new and therefore not of great historical significance, it is in fact the second most important temple in Bali after Pura Besakih. As Stephen Lansing explains in his book *Priests and Programmers* (1991), the Goddess of the Crater Lake is honoured here and symbolically the temple controls water for all the island's irrigation systems. Ultimately, therefore, it controls the livelihoods of the majority of the population. A nine-tiered meru honours the goddess and unlike other temples it is open 24 hours a day. A virgin priestess still selects 24 boys as priests, who remain tied as servants of the temple for the rest of their lives.

Pura Tegeh Koripan
ⓘ *Daily, 6000Rp, catch a bemo running north and get off at Penulisan.*
Pura Tegeh Koripan is the last place on the crater rim, on the main road 200 m north of Penulisan. Steep stairs (333 in all) lead up to the temple, which stands at a height of over 1700 m above sea level next to a broadcasting mast. The temple contains a number of weathered statues, thought to be portraits of royalty. They are dated between 1011 and 1335. Artistically they are surprising because they seem to anticipate later Majapahit works. The whole place is run-down at the moment, though there are some signs that repairs are being attempted.

Alternative routes from Ubud to Gunung Batur
If you have your own transport and are starting from Ubud, you can turn left at the end of Ubud's main street and take the back road heading north. This leads through an almost continuous ribbon of craft villages, mainly specializing in woodcarving, with pieces ranging in size from chains of monkeys to full size doors and 2-m-high *garudas*. There are good bargains to be found in this area off the main tourist track. Follow the road through **Petulu**, **Sapat** and **Tegalalong**, and continue northwards. The road, its surface not too good in places, climbs steadily through rice paddies and then more open countryside where cows and goats graze, before eventually arriving at the crater rim – 500 m west of Penelokan.

The area around Gunung Batur is considered very sacred and comprises numerous temples, small pretty villages and countryside consisting of rice fields littered with volcanic debris. There are several rugged backroutes from Ubud through this region. One of the most interesting villages is **Sebatu**, northeast of Ubud near Pura Mount Kawi, reached via a small road leading east from the northern end of **Pujung Kelod**. This village has a number of temples and is renowned for the refined quality of its dance troupe, its *gamelan* orchestra and its woodcarving. The dance troupe has revived several unusual traditional dances including the *telek* dance and makes regular appearances overseas. **Pura Gunung Kawi** is a water temple with well-maintained shrines and pavilions, a pool fed by an underground spring and open air public bathing.

From Gunung Batur to the north coast

From Penulisan, the main road runs down to the north coast, which it joins at **Kubutambahan**. It is a long descent as the road twists down the steep hillsides, and there are many hairpin bends.

If exploring the northeast coast, a very pleasant alternative is to take the minor road that turns directly north, just short of a small village called **Dusa**. The turning is not well signed – ask to make sure you are on the right road.

This is a steep descent but the road is well made and quiet. It follows ridges down from the crater of Gunung Batur, with steep drops into ravines on either side. The route passes through clove plantations and small friendly villages, with stupendous views to the north over the sea. Behind, the tree-covered slopes lead back up to the crater.

The road eventually joins the coast road near Tegakula. Turn left, northwest, for Singaraja and Lovina, and right, southeast, for the road to Amlapura.

Gianyar to Gunung Batur via Bangli listings

For Sleeping and Eating price codes and other relevant information, see pages 7-10.

😴 Sleeping

Bangli *p57*
$$-$ Artha Sastra Inn, Jln Merdeka 5, T0366 91179. Offers 14 rooms. Located in the inner court of the royal palace with plenty of atmosphere, although don't expect anything too grand. This is the place to stay in Bangli. The more expensive rooms are clean, simple, with private bathroom and Western toilet; cheaper rooms have shared *mandis* with squat toilets. Restaurant (**$**).
$ Catur Aduyana Homestay, Jln Lettu Lila 2, T0366 91244. Clean and pleasant homestay located 1 km to the south of the town centre. 7 rooms: 3 with private *mandi*, squat toilet, 4 with shared *mandi*, squat toilet.

Breakfast of tea/coffee and bread included. Friendly owner speaks no English.
$ Losmen Dharma Putra. A good, friendly, family-run *losmen*, price includes breakfast.

Gunung Batur *p59*
$$ The Art Centre (or *Balai Seni*), Toya Bungkah. Quite old but still good.
$ Under the Volcano, Toya Bungkah, T081 3386 0081. Clean rooms, friendly management, good restaurant.

Penelokan *p61*
$$$ Lakeview Hotel, Jln Raya Penelokan, T0361 728790 (Bali office), www.indo.com/hotels/lakeview. Basic, comfortable and with good views all the way to Lombok. Good online discounts available
$$ Gunawan Losmen. Clean, private bathroom, fantastic position.

Kintamani p61
$$ Hotel Surya, Jln Kedisan, T0366 51139, www.suryahotel.com. In a great position, comfortable rooms.
$$ Losmen Sasaka. Stunning views.
$$ Puri Astina. Large clean rooms.

🍴 Eating

Bangli p57
There are *warungs* beside the bemo station in the centre of town, and a good night market opposite the **Artha Sastra Inn**, with the usual staple Indonesian/Balinese stall food including noodles, rice, *nasi campur*, *sate*, etc. Near the **Catur Aduyana Homestay**, opposite **Yunika**, is a clean **Rumah Makan**. Foodstalls near the Pura Kehan sell simple snacks.

🎭 Entertainment

Gianyar p57
At 1900 every Mon and Thu, a cultural show including dinner is staged at the **Agung Gianyar Palace**, T0361 93943/51654.

▲▲ Activities and tours

Perama has a guided trek starting at 0300 from Pura Jati, on the edge of Danau Batur and reaching the peak in time for sunrise. US$60 per person (minimum 2 people), including transfers to and from Kuta, Ubud and Sanur. Or, you can arrange your own trek from Toya Bungka, using a local guide. It should cost around US$40-50 for a 4- to 5-hr trek to the summit and back. Bargain hard. The guides will find you. This can be annoying, and makes the prospect of the hassle-free **Perama** package look enticing.

Gianyar p57
Mountain biking
Sobek Expeditions, T0361 287059, www.balisobek.com. Organizes rides down into the volcano on the 'Batur Trail'. US$79 adult, US$52 chid.

⊖ Transport

Gianyar p57
Bemo
Regular connections with **Denpasar**'s Batubulan terminal.

Bus
To **Semmarapura** (25 mins), **Padangbai** (50 mins) and **Candi Dasi** (1 hr 10 mins).

Bangli p57
Bemo
Many (but not all) bemos are 'colour coded'. Bemos run throughout the day, and most places are accessible by bemo if you are prepared to wait and do some walking. There are services between: **Denpasar**'s Batubulan terminal, many connect through to **Singaraja**; the market in **Gianyar** (these bemos are usually blue); and **Semarapura**. Blue bemos wait at the Bangli intersection on the main road between Gianyar and Semarapura at Peteluan; so it's easy to change bemos here. The road climbs steadily up to Bangli with good views to the south. Generally, orange bemos run from Bangli to **Kintamani**. To **Rendang** they are generally black or brown and white. Bemos also run between **Besakih** and to **Amlapura**. All fairly regularly from 0600-1700; fewer in the afternoon. The road from Bangli to Rendang is good but winding, with little traffic; it is also pretty with ravines, streams and overhead viaducts made of bamboo and concrete.

Trunyan p60
Bemo
From **Denpasar**'s Batubulan terminal to **Bangli** and then another to **Penelokan**. Some bemos drive down into the crater to **Kedisan** and **Toya Bungkah**.

Bus
Regular coach services from **Denpasar** (2-3 hrs).

● Directory

Bangli *p57*

Banks Several, including **Bank Rakyat Indonesia**, Jln Kusuma Yudha, T0366 91019, in the centre of town by the Bale Kulkul.

Medical services General Hospital, Jln Kusuma Yudha 27, T0366 91020. Pharmacy: Apotik Kurnia Farma, Jln Kusuma Yudha, and in Toko Obat Rhizoma, Jln Bridjen Ngurah Rai.

Post office Jln Kusuma Yudha 18.

Pura Besakih and Gunung Agung

The holiest and most important temple on Bali is Pura Besakih, situated on the slopes of Bali's sacred Gunung Agung. Twinned with Gunung Batur to the northwest, Agung is the highest mountain on the island, rising to 3140 m. It is easiest to approach Besakih by taking the road north from Semarapura, a distance of 22 km. However, there are also two east–west roads, linking the Semarapura route to Besakih with Bangli in the west and Amlapura in the east. Although little public transport uses these routes, they are among the most beautiful drives in Bali, through verdant terraced rice paddies.

Pura Besakih

Pura Besakih is a complex of 22 *puras* that lie scattered over the south slopes of Gunung Agung, at an altitude of about 950 m. Of these, the largest and most important is the Pura Penataran Agung, the Mother Temple of Bali. It is here that every Balinese can come to worship – although in the past it was reserved for the royal families of Semarapura, Karangkasem and Bangli. The other 21 temples that sprawl across the slopes of Gunung Agung surrounding the Mother Temple are linked to particular clans. **Gunung Agung** last erupted in 1963, killing 2000 people. The area has been sacred for several centuries.

The **Pura Penataran Agung**, which most visitors refer to as Pura Besakih, is dedicated to Siva and is of great antiquity.

Ins and outs
The site is open daily from 0800 until sunset and entrance costs 10000Rp plus 1000Rp for a camera. There is another ticket office on the climb up the hill where you have to sign in and are invited to make a further donation (ignore the vast sums that are claimed to have been donated). Guides are available for around 25,000Rp. The best time to visit is early in the morning, before the tour groups arrive.

Getting there Besakih is 22 km from Semarapura and 60 km from Denpasar, with regular minibus services from both. From Denpasar catch a bemo from the Batubulan terminal to Semarapura, and then get a connection on to Besakih (via Rendang). However, bemos are irregular for this final leg of the journey and it makes more sense to charter a bemo for the entire trip, or rent a car or motorbike (chartering a bemo makes good sense in a group).

Temple layout
From the entrance gate, it is a 10-minute walk up to the temple. Although you can walk up and around the sides of the temple, the courtyards are only open to worshippers. It is the position of this *pura* that makes it special: there are views to the waters of the Lombok Strait.

Pura Besakih consists of three distinct sections (also see box, above). The entrance to the forecourt is through a *candi bentar* or split gate, immediately in front of which –

Balinese pura

In Bali there are more than 20,000 *pura* (temples) – and most villages have at least three. The *pura puseh*, (navel temple), is the village-origin temple where the village ancestors are worshipped. The *pura dalem* (temple of the dead) is usually near the cremation ground. The *pura bale agung* is the temple of the great assembly hall and is used for meetings of the village. There are also irrigation temples, temples at particular geographical sites, and the six great temples or *sadkahyangan*.

There are nine directional temples, *kayangan jagat*, found at notable geographical sites around the island, particularly on mountains, on imposing outcrops overlooking the sea and beside lakes. These are among the most sacred temples on Bali and their strategic locations have been chosen to ensure that they safeguard the island. Besakih, high on the slopes of Bali's most sacred and highest mountain, Gunung Agung, is the preeminent of these directional temples and corresponds to the ninth directional point (the centre). The others, of equal importance, guard the other eight directions. From the southwest they are: Pura Luhur Uluwatu, **Pura Luhur Batukau** (on Mount Batukau), **Pura Ulun Danu Batur** (high on edge of the crater of Mount Batur; this temple used to be beside the lake, but eruptions in 1917 and 1926 caused so much destruction that it was moved, **Pura Ulun Danu Bratan** (beside Lake Bratan), **Pura Pasar Agung** (near Selat on the slopes of Mount Agung), **Pura Lempuyang** (on Mount Lempuyang near Tirtagangga), **Pura Goa Lawah** (near Padangbai), **Pura Masceti** (near Lebi), and the mother temple, Pura Besakih. Balinese visit the *kayangan jagat* nearest their home at the time of its *odalan*, anniversary festival, to seek protection and make offerings to the spirits.

Balinese *pura* are places where evil spirits are rendered harmless, but gods must be appeased and courted if they are to protect people, so offerings are brought. The temple buildings are less important than the ground, which is consecrated.

The temple complex consists of three courts (two in north Bali), each separated by walls: the front court, or *jaba*, the central court, or *jaba tengah*, and the inner court, or *jeroan*. The innermost court is the most sacred and is thought to represent heaven; the outermost, the underworld; and the central court, an intermediate place.

unusually for Bali – is a *bale pegat*, which symbolizes the cutting of the material from the heavenly worlds. Also here is the *bale kulkul*, a pavilion for the wooden split gongs. At the far end of this first courtyard are two *bale mundar-mandir* or *bale ongkara*.

Entering the central courtyard, almost directly in front of the gateway, is the *bale pewerdayan*. This is the spot where the priests recite the sacred texts. On the left-hand wall is the *pegongan*, a pavilion where a *gamelan* orchestra plays during ceremonies. Along the opposite (right-hand) side of the courtyard is the large *bale agung*, where meetings of the Besakih village are held. The small *panggungan* or altar, in front and at the near end of the *bale agung*, is used to present offerings. The similar *bale pepelik* at the far end is the altar used to present offerings to the Hindu trinity – Vishnu, Brahma and Siva. These gods descend and assemble in the larger *sanggar agung*, which lies in front of the *bale pepelik*.

From the central courtyard, a steep stone stairway leads to the upper section, which is arranged into four terraces. The first of these in the inner courtyard is split into an east

Note Macaques at temple sites should not be teased, fed, or purchased.

Balinese pura layout
The outer court or jaba
The entrance to the *jaba* is usually through a candi bentar, (split temple) gate – if the two halves of the gate are pushed together, closing the entranceway, they would form the shape of a complete *candi*.

Within the *jaba* are a number of structures. In one corner is the *bale kulkul* (*bale* pavilion, *kulkul* wooden gong), a pavilion in which hangs a large hollow, wooden, gong or drum. The *kulkul* is beaten during temple ceremonies and also in times of emergency or disaster – during an earthquake, for example. Also within the *jaba*, it is not uncommon to find a *jineng* – a small barn used to store rice produced from the temple's own fields (*laba pura*).

The central court or jaba tengah
The entrance leading to the central court is through the *candi kurung*. This is also in the form of a *candi*, but in this case a wooden doorway allows visitors to pass through. In a village *pura*, the centre of the *jaba tengah* will be dominated by an open pavilion with a roof of grass or reed. This is the *bale agung* or village conference hall. There is also often a *bale* for pilgrims who wish to stay overnight in the temple.

The inner court or jeroan
The entrance to the inner court is through a second, larger, *candi kurung* called the *paduraksa*. The entrance is usually guarded by a demon's head and rises up in the form of a pyramid. In larger temples, there may be three gateways. Along the back wall of the jeroan are the most sacred of the shrines. These may have multiple roofs – as many as 11. The greater the number of roofs, the more important the god. Also on the back wall, there is a stone pillar or *tugu*. It is at the *tugu* that offerings are left for the *taksu*, the god whose job it is to protect the temple and through whom the wishes of the gods are transmitted to the dancer during a trance dance. In the centre of the jeroan is the *parungan* or *pepelik* – the seat of all the gods, where they assemble during temple ceremonies. Finally, along the right-hand wall of the inner courtyard, are two *sanggahs* – Ngurah Gde and Ngurah Alit. These are the 'secretaries' of the gods; they ensure that temple offerings are properly prepared. (Condensed from: East Utrecht and B Hering (1986), *The temples of Bali*.)

(right) and west (left) half. To the right are two large *merus*; the *meru* with the seven-tiered roof is dedicated to the god Ratu Geng, while the 11-tiered *meru* is dedicated to Ratu Mas. The three-tiered *kehen meru* is used to store the temple treasures. On the left-hand side is a row of four *merus* and two stone altars. The tallest *meru*, with seven tiers, is dedicated to Ida Batara Tulus Sadewa. Up some steps, on the second terrace, is another 11-tiered *meru*, this one dedicated to Ratu Sunar ing Jagat (Lord Light of the World). There are also a number of *bale* here; the *bale* in a separate enclosure to the left is dedicated to Sira Empu, the patron god of blacksmiths. Up to the third terrace is a further 11-tiered *meru*, dedicated to Batara Wisesa. On the final terrace are two *gedongs* – covered buildings enclosed on all four sides – dedicated to the god of Gunung Agung.

At the back of the complex there is a path leading to three other major *puras*: **Gelap** (200 m), **Pengubengan** (2.5 km) and **Tirta** (2 km). There are over 20 temples on these terraced slopes, dedicated to every Hindu god in the pantheon.

Festivals

Seventy festivals are held around Pura Besakih each year, with every shrine having its own festival. The two most important festivals are occasional ceremonies: the **Panca Wali Krama** is held every 10 years, while the **Eka Dasa Rudra** is held only once every 100 years and lasts for two months. Two **Eka Dasa Rudra** festivals have been held this century. In March or April is the movable festival of **Nyepi** (on the full moon of 10th lunar month), the Balinese Saka new year, a month-long festival attended by thousands of people from all over Bali.

Gunung Agung

Gunung Agung is Bali's tallest and most sacred mountain, home of the Hindu gods and dwelling place of the ancestral spirits, it dominates the spiritual and physical life of the island. All directions on Bali are given in relation to this much revered mountain. Toward the mountain is called '*kaja*', away from the mountain is '*kelod*'. This is the site of the most important of the nine directional temples (see box, page 66). Water from its sacred springs is the holiest and most sought after for temple rites. According to local legend, the god Pasupati created the mountain by dividing Mount Mahmeru, centre of the Hindu universe, in two – making Gunung Agung and Gunung Batur.

Standing 3014 m high, at its summit is a crater about 500 m in width. In 1969, after lying dormant for more than 600 years, the volcano erupted causing massive destruction; over 1600 people died in the eruption, a further 500 in the aftermath and 9000 were made homeless. Even today the scars left by the destruction are visible in the shape of lava flows and ravines. Much was read into the fact that the eruption took place at the time of Bali's greatest religious festival, **Eka Dasa Rudra** (see above). One theory is that the mountain erupted because the priests were pressured into holding the ceremony before due time, to coincide with an important tourism convention that was taking place on Bali.

Climbing Gunung Agung

Gunung Agung is a sacred mountain, so access is restricted during religious ceremonies, particularly in March and April. The arduous climb should only be attempted during the dry season, May to October; even then conditions on the summit can be quite different from the coast. There are several routes up Gunung Agung, but the two most popular depart from Besakih and Selat. You should be well prepared; the mountain is cold at night and you will need warm clothes, water, food, a good torch and decent footwear. You will also need a guide, and should aim to reach the summit before 0700 to witness the spectacular sunrise.

From Besakih The route takes you to the summit, providing the best views in all directions. The longer of the two ascents, this climb takes about six hours, with another four to five hours for the demanding descent. You start out in forest, but once you reach the open mountain it becomes extremely steep. The tourist office at Besakih hires guides (about US$60 per person, including temple offerings) and can arrange accommodation.

From Selat This route reaches a point about 100 m below the summit, which obscures all-round views. However, the climb only takes three to four hours; aim to set off by 0330. From Selat, take the road to Pura Pasar Agung, then climb through forest before reaching the bare mountain. Guides can be arranged in Muncan, Tirtagangga or Selat. A recommended guide is **I Ketut Uriada**, a teacher who lives in Muncan; he can be contacted at his shop in that village, T0812 364 6426. Costs start at about US$50, which includes temple contributions and registering with the local police. In Selat ask the police about guides, they should be able to advise. In Tirtagangga ask at your accommodation; rates here tend to be around US$50 per person, which should include transport. There is accommodation in Selat, or your guide may arrange cheaper lodgings at his home. **Perama** ① *T0361 751875 in Kuta, T0361 973316 in Ubud*, offers a one-night two-day trek up Gunung Agung including visits to Kamasan, Kertagosa and Sideman, where the climb begins at 0100. The four-hour trek arrives in time for sunrise on the summit. Transfers to and from Kuta, Ubud and Sanur are included in the price (US$100 per person – minimum two people).

East Bali, Karangasem and the north coast

The greatest of the former principalities of Bali is Semarapura (formerly Klungkung), and its capital still has a number of sights that hint at its former glory. It is worth driving east of here into the Regency of Karangasem: to the ancient Bali Aga village of Tenganan, 3 km outside Candi Dasa, then inland and northeast to Amlapura (Karangkasem), with its royal palace, then 7 km north to the royal bathing pools of Tirtagangga. From here the road continues north, following the coast all the way to Singaraja (almost 100 km from Amlapura). The drive is very beautiful, passing black-sand beaches and coconut groves.

An area of great beauty dominated by Gunung Agung (3140 m), Bali's highest and most sacred volcano, Karangasem is one of the most traditional parts of Bali and one of the most rewarding areas to explore. During the 17th and 18th centuries, Karangasem was the most powerful kingdom on Bali. Its sphere of influence extended to western Lombok, and the cross-cultural exchanges that resulted endure to this day. During the 19th century, the regency cooperated with the Dutch, thus ensuring its continued prosperity.

The massive eruption of Gunung Agung in 1963 devastated much of the regency and traces of the lava flows can still be seen along the northeast coast, particularly north of Tulamben.

Ins and outs

Getting there
By bus Buses run most frequently in the morning starting early (from 0500 or 0600), and continue until about 1700. Buses from Denpasar (Batubulan terminal) run to Semarapura (1¼ hours), Padangbai (one hour 50 minutes) and Candi Dasa (two hours 10 minutes). There are also regular bus connections from Gianyar.

Several companies run tourist shuttle buses linking Padangbai, Candi Dasa, Tirtagangga and Tulemben with Ubud, Kuta, Sanur (and Nusa Lembongan by boat), Kintamani, Lovina, Bedugul and Air Sanih; as well as Mataram, Bangsal, the Gili Islands, Kuta Lombok and Tetebatu on Lombok. One of the best is **Perama**, with offices in all the above places; allow three hours to get to Denpasar airport from Candi Dasa.

Note All times are approximate and can vary enormously depending on traffic conditions from Denpasar, particularly on the main road from Semarapura to Denpasar.

By boat From Padangbai there is a 24-hour ferry service (leaving every two hours) to Lembar port on Lombok (four to five hours). There is also a fast ferry service direct from Padangbai to the Gili Islands off Lombok.

Getting around
While you can reach most of these villages by public bemo, it is better to hire a car. There are many scenic backroads that climb up into the hills, offering spectacular views when the weather is fine. Be warned that some of these minor roads are in dreadful condition with numerous, huge potholes. The road leading up from Perasi through Timbrah and Bungaya to Bebandem is especially scenic and potholed. A much better road with outstanding views leads west from Amlapura to Rendang; en route you pass through an area famed for its salak fruit and in the vicinity of Muncan you will find beautiful rice terraces. From Rendang you can continue on up to Pura Besakih.

Semarapura and around → *For listings, see pages 79-89. Phone code: 0366.*

The **Puri Semarapura** was the symbolic heart of the kingdom of Semarapura. All that remains of this palace on Jalan Untung Surapati are the gardens and two buildings; the rest was destroyed in 1908 by the Dutch during their advance on the capital and the ensuing *puputan*. The **Kherta Ghosa** (Hall of Justice), built in the 18th century by Ida Dewa Agung Jambe, was formerly the supreme court of the Kingdom of Semarapura. It is famous for its ceiling murals painted in traditional, *wayang* style, with illustrations of heaven (towards the top) and hell (on the lower panels). As a court, the paintings represent the punishment that awaits a criminal in the afterlife. The murals have been repainted several times this century. Miguel Covarrubias describes the nature of traditional justice in Bali in the following terms:

"A trial must be conducted with the greatest dignity and restraint. There are rules for the language employed, the behaviour of the participants, and the payment of trial expenses ... On the appointed day the plaintiff and the defendant must appear properly dressed, with their witnesses and their cases and declarations carefully written down ... When the case has been thoroughly stated, the witnesses have testified and the evidence has been produced, the judges study the statements and go into deliberation among themselves until they reach a decision. Besides the witnesses and the material evidence, special attention is paid to the physical reaction of the participants during the trial, such as nervousness, change of colour in the face, or hard breathing."

The Kherta Ghosa was transformed into a Western court by the Dutch in 1908, when they added the carved seats, as they found sitting on mats too uncomfortable. It is said – although the story sounds rather dubious – that one of the Rajahs of Semarapura used the Kherta Ghosa as a watch tower. He would look over the town and when his eyes alighted on a particularly attractive woman going to the temple to make offerings, he would order his guards to fetch her and add the unsuspecting maid to his collection of wives.

Adjoining the Kherta Ghosa is the **Bale Kambangg** (Floating Pavilion), originally built in the 18th century, but extensively restored since then. Like the Kherta Ghosa, the ceiling is painted with murals; these date from 1942.

Further along the same road, just past a school, is the attractive **Taman Gili** ① *6000Rp*, also built in the 18th century. This consists of a series of open courtyards with finely carved stonework, in the centre of which is a floating pavilion surrounded by a lotus-filled moat.

To the east of the main crossroads in the centre of town – behind the shop fronts – is a bustling **market**, held here every three days and considered by many to be the best market on Bali, and also a large monument commemorating the *puputan*.

Kamasan village
Four kilometres southeast of Semarapura is an important arts centre where artists still practise the classical *wayang*-style of painting. Most of the artist families live in the Banjar Sangging area of town. Artists from this village painted the original ceiling in the Kerta Gosa in Semarapura in the 18th century, as well as the recent restoration, using the muted natural colours (reds, blacks, blues, greens and ochres) typical of this school.

Goa Lawah
① *Take a bemo heading for Padangbai or Candi Dasa.*
Goa Lawah, (Bat Cave), is one of the state temples of Semarapura, with tunnels that are reputed to lead as far as Pura Besakih. The temple is overrun by bats and their smells.

Kusamba
Boats leave for **Nusa Penida** and **Nusa Lembongan** from the fishing village of Kusamba, 8 km southeast from Semarapura. On the beach are huts and shallow troughs used in salt production. The fishing fleet consists of hundreds of brightly painted outrigger craft with triangular sails, which operate in the Lombok Strait (similar to the *lis-alis* of Madura). They are fast and manoeuvrable, and can make way in even the lightest breezes.

Tirtagangga
① *6000Rp adult.*
Seven kilometres northwest of Semarapura is the site of the royal bathing pools of Tirtagangga. The pools are set on a beautiful position on the side of a hill, overlooking terraced rice fields. The complex is composed of various pools (some of which can be swum in; enquire at the entrance gate) fed by mountain springs, with water spouting from fountains and animals carved from stone. It is popular with locals as well as foreign visitors, and is a peaceful spot to relax during the week, although those seeking tranquillity are advised not to visit at weekends when the place is overrun with domestic tourists. There are a couple of places to stay, and a few restaurants.

Amed → *Phone code: 0363.*
For peace and quiet, this area on the east coast, north of Tirtagangga, has much to offer. The drive from Culik via Amed to **Lipah Beach** is quite spectacular, especially on the return journey, with Gunung Agung forming a magnificent backdrop to the coastal scenery. Numerous coves and headlands, with colourful fishing boats, complete the vista and offer endless possibilities for walks and picnics. The area became popular because of the good snorkelling and diving available here, the reef is just 10 m from the beach with some good coral and a variety of fish. Amed is developing slowly with new guesthouses, hotels, restaurants and dive centres opening every year, some with spectacular hillside locations and stunning views of Gunung Agung. At present much of the accommodation lies beyond Amed on the stretch from Jemeluk to Bunutan.

The area called Amed is in fact a 15-km stretch from Culik to Selang village, encompassing the villages of **Amed**, **Cemeluk** (also spelt Jemeluk), **Bunutan** and **Selang**. At present the first accommodation you come to is 5.7 km from Culik. If you go during the dry season you can watch the local men making salt; they also work year round as fishermen, setting off at 0500 and returning about 1000, and then going out again at 1500. It is possible to go out with them. As there is no irrigation system, farming is mainly done in the wet season when the men raise crops of peanuts, corn, pumpkin and beans, on the steeply sloping hillside inland from the road, to sell in the market at Amlapura. In dry spells, all the water needed for the crops is carried by the women up the steep slope, three times a day; a back-breaking chore. Most of the land is communally owned by the local Banjar.

Padangbai → For listings, see pages 79-89. Phone code: 0363.

Padangbai has a beautiful setting, overlooking a crescent-shaped bay with golden sand beach, colourful *jukung* (fishing boats) and surrounded by verdant hills. This is the port for ferries to Lombok and boats to Nusa Penida, and is a hive of excitement when ferries arrive and depart. It is one of the best deep-water harbours in Bali. There are beaches on either side of the town. Walking south from the pier and bus station, follow the road until you come to a tatty sign on the left indicating the rough, steep path that leads up and over the hill to **Pantai Cecil** (400 m). This is a beautiful, white-sand beach, the perfect setting for a quiet swim or evening stroll. There are two beachside *warungs*. Unfortunately, the once-verdant hills behind the beach have been consumed by a development of luxury villas.

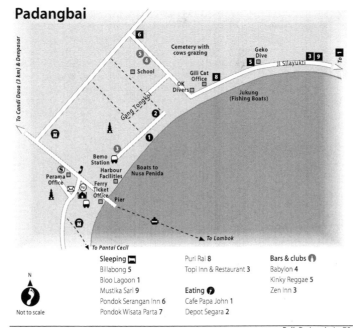

Padangbai

Not to scale

Sleeping	Puri Rai 8	Bars & clubs
Billabong 5	Topi Inn & Restaurant 3	Babylon 4
Bloo Lagoon 1		Kinky Reggae 5
Mustika Sari 9	Eating	Zen Inn 3
Pondok Serangan Inn 6	Cafe Papa John 1	
Pondok Wisata Parta 7	Depot Segara 2	

The beach maintains its beauty, but the ambience is nowhere near as relaxed as it was. The walk over the headland has good views of the town and hills beyond.

Padangbai to Candi Dasa

For many people Bali is at its best and most rewarding away from the tourist centres. Along the road leading from Padangbai to Candi Dasa there are several hotels and bungalow-style accommodation, which offer peace and quiet in secluded settings with beautiful sea views. Breakfast is included in the price except at the luxury hotels.

Manggis and Balina Beach Balina Beach lies midway between Padangbai and Candi Dasa (approximately 4 km from the latter) adjacent to the village of Buitan, which runs this tourist development as a cooperative for the benefit of the villagers. It is a slightly scruffy black-sand beach with a definite tourist feel to it. **Sengkidu** village and beach 2 km further east have more charm. Sometimes there are strong currents.

The village of **Buitan** has a public telephone, several small *warungs* and shops; the road to the beach and the accommodation is signposted. Perhaps the highlight of this village is the large advertisement promoting the advantages of artificial insemination in pig breeding. The village of **Manggis**, inland and to the west of Buitan, is known locally for its associations with black magic; it is said to be the haunt of *leyaks*, witches with supernatural powers. There is a road from here leading up to **Putung**, 6 km away, with spectacular views over the Lombok Strait.

Candi Dasa → *For listings, see pages 79-89. Phone code: 0363.*

Candi Dasa is smaller, more intimate and offers better value for money than the main resorts of Bali. It is also an excellent base from which to explore the sights of East Bali.

The gold- and black-sand beach has been badly eroded and beach lovers will be disappointed. However, the government is pouring in money to create a new man-made beach at the western end of the development to try and regain some of the area's undoubted lost glory.

Candi Dasa gets its name from the **temple** on the hill overlooking the main road and the freshwater lagoon; the ancient relics in this temple indicate that there has been a village on this site since the 11th century.

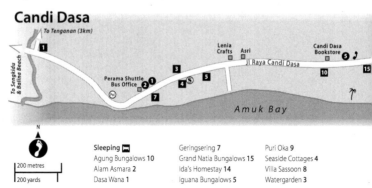

Candi Dasa

Sleeping		
Agung Bungalows 10	Geringsering 7	Puri Oka 9
Alam Asmara 2	Grand Natia Bungalows 15	Seaside Cottages 4
Dasa Wana 1	Ida's Homestay 14	Villa Sassoon 8
	Iguana Bungalows 5	Watergarden 3

Traditionally fishermen in these parts have gone out fishing each day from 0400 until 0800, and again from about 1430 until 1800. Although most people on Bali fear the sea as a place of evil spirits and a potential source of disaster, those who live near the sea and earn their living from it consider it a holy place and worship such sea gods as Baruna. The boats they use, *jukung*, are made from locally grown wood and bamboo, which is cut according to traditional practice. The day chosen for cutting down the tree must be deemed favourable by the gods to whom prayers and offerings are then made, and a sapling is planted to replace it. Carved from a single tree trunk without using nails and with bamboo outriders to give it stability, the finished boat will be gaily coloured with the characteristic large eyes that enable it to see where the fish lurk. The design has not changed for thousands of years; it is very stable due to the low centre of gravity created by the way the sail is fastened. These days there are fewer fish to catch and many fishermen take tourists out snorkelling. *Jukungs* cost about US$40 to hire for a couple of hours.

In the rice field by the road to Tenganan are two ingenious **bird-scaring devices**, operated by a man sitting in a thatched hut. One is a metre-long bamboo pole with plastic bags and strips of bamboo; when the man pulls on the attached rope, the pole swings round, causing the bamboo strips to make a clacking noise and the plastic bags to flutter. The other consists of two 4-m-long bamboo poles that are hinged at one end, with flags and plastic bags attached; when the attached rope is pulled, the two poles swing round with flags and plastic bags waving.

Tenganan

ⓘ *Admission to the village is by donation, vehicles prohibited. It is possible to walk the 3 km from Candi Dasa; take the road heading north, 1 km to the west of Candi Dasa – it ends at the village. Alternatively, walk or catch a bemo heading west towards Semarapura, get off at the turning 1 km west of Candi Dasa and catch an ojek up to the village. Tours to Tenganan are also arranged by the bigger hotels and the tour agents on the main road. Bemos run past the turn-off for the village from Denpasar's Batubulan terminal.*

This village is reputed to be the oldest on Bali, and is a village of the Bali Aga, the island's original inhabitants before the Hindu invasion almost 1000 years ago (see box, page 60). The walled community consists of a number of longhouses, rice barns, shrines, pavilions and a large village meeting hall, all arranged in accordance with traditional beliefs.

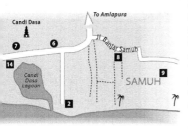

Membership of the village is exclusive and until recently visitors were actively discouraged. The inhabitants have to have been born here and marry within the village; anyone who violates the rules is banished to a neighbouring community. Despite the studied maintenance of a traditional way of life, the inhabitants of Tenganan have decided to embrace the tourist industry. It is in fact a very wealthy village, deriving income not only from tourism but also from a large area of communally owned and worked rice paddies and dryland fields.

Tenganan is one of the last villages to produce the unusual **double ikat** or

Eating 🍴
Candi Dasa Cafe 1
Ganesha 2
Kubu Bali 5

Raja's 6
Srijati 7
Toke 2

geringsing, where both the warp and the weft are tie-dyed, and great skill is needed to align and then weave the two into the desired pattern. The cloth is woven on body-tension (back-strap) looms with a continuous warp; colours used are dark rust, brown and purple, although newer pieces suffer from fading due to the use of inferior dyes. Motifs are floral and geometric, and designs are constrained to about 20 traditional forms. It is said that one piece of cloth takes about five years to complete and only six families still understand the process. **Note** Much of the cloth for sale in the village does not originate from Tenganan.

About 13 km southwest of Candi Dasa is the temple and cave of **Goa Lawah**, see page 72.

Around Candi Dasa

The town and palace of **Amlapura** is within easy reach of Candi Dasa. Three small islands with coral reefs are to be found 30 minutes by boat from Candi Dasa. They make a good day trip for snorkelling or diving. Samuh village cooperative keeps goats on the largest of these islands, called **Nusa Kambing (Goat Island)** ① *most hotels and losmen will arrange a boat for the day*. Every six months the goats are transported back to the mainland by boat. Quite a sight if you are lucky enough to witness it.

Sengkidu village → *Phone code: 0366.*

West of Candi Dasa (2 km) is an authentic Balinese village as yet unravaged by tourism. The pretty backstreets lead down to the sea and beach. Surrounded by coconut groves and tropical trees, Sengkidu offers an attractive alternative to Candi Dasa. The village itself has a number of shops, fruit stalls and a temple where festivals are celebrated; foreigners are welcome to participate if they observe temple etiquette and wear the appropriate dress, otherwise they can watch.

Lovina → *For listings, see pages 79-89. Phone code: 0362.*

Lovina, an 8-km stretch of grey sand, is the name given to an area that begins 7 km west of Singaraja and includes six villages. From east to west they are **Pemaron**, **Tukad Mungga**, **Anturan**, **Kalibukbuk**, **Kaliasem** and **Temukus**, all merging into each other. Lovina is one of the larger beach resorts on Bali and caters to all ages and price groups, from backpackers to package tour-oriented clientele. Kalibukbuk is the heart of Lovina, the busiest, most developed part, with the greatest number of tourist facilities and nightlife. Lying 1 km to the east of Kalibukbuk, **Banyualit** has a number of peaceful hotels scattered along the shoreline. There are also a couple of hotels slightly inland here, some of which are fair value.

Recent times have been hard on Lovina, with tourist arrivals a mere trickle of what they were a few years ago. Local residents blame the bomb attacks in Bali for the low numbers, and many lament the tough competition they face in gaining customers. For visitors, the upside of this situation is the great deals that can be had at empty hotels. Lovina has a relaxed pace of life and the inhabitants are friendly and welcoming. It's a great place to linger and make a local friend or two.

The beach

The beach itself is quite narrow in places and the grey/black sand is not the prettiest, but the waters are calm, so swimming is very safe and there is reasonable snorkelling on the reef just offshore. The beach is interspersed with streams running into the sea, where some villagers wash in the evening. Several areas are the preserve of local fishermen whose dogs can be menacing if you are out for a walk, particularly in the evening. Hawkers are not as bad as they used to be but can still be a nuisance, and it seems as if the entire resort is on commission for the much-touted dolphin trips.

The most popular outing is an early morning boat trip to see the **dolphins** cavorting off the coast; there are two schools of dolphin that regularly swim there. In the Kalibukbuk area the fishermen run a cooperative that fixes the number of people in each boat and the price, currently 75,000Rp; snorkelling is not included in the price. If you book through your hotel you will pay more for the convenience, but the price may include refreshments and the opportunity to go snorkelling afterwards. Boats set off at about 0600 and the tour usually lasts 1½ hours. Bear in mind that there is no shade on the boats. People have mixed reactions to the experience. If yours is the first boat to reach the dolphin area then you may be rewarded with 12 dolphins leaping and playing, but as other boats arrive the dolphins may be chased away. It is worth bearing in mind that around Lombok, and further east, dolphins can often be seen leaping out of the water alongside ferries and boats.

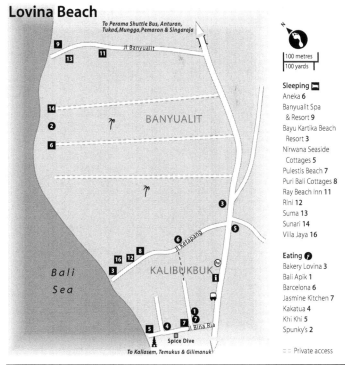

Lovina Beach

Sleeping 🛏
Aneka **6**
Banyualit Spa
 & Resort **9**
Bayu Kartika Beach
 Resort **3**
Nirwana Seaside
 Cottages **5**
Pulestis Beach **7**
Puri Bali Cottages **8**
Ray Beach Inn **11**
Rini **12**
Suma **13**
Sunari **14**
Villa Jaya **16**

Eating 🍴
Bakery Lovina **3**
Bali Apik **1**
Barcelona **6**
Jasmine Kitchen **7**
Kakatua **4**
Khi Khi **5**
Spunky's **2**

= = Private access

Bull races

Bull races, *sapi gerumbungan*, take place on Independence Day, 17 August, and on some other national holidays such as Singaraja Day, 31 March, check exact dates at the tourist office. The Balinese name for the races is derived from the huge wooden bells *gerumbungan*, which the bulls (*sapi* in Indonesian) wear around their necks during the races. These bull races are unique to Buleleng and originated as a religious ceremony to propitiate the gods before planting the new rice crop. The specially trained bulls, decorated with colourful ornaments and silk banners, and with equally well-dressed drivers, were originally raced over a flooded ricefield, usefully ploughing the field as they competed. Recently the event has been held on playing fields in the village of Kaliasem to the west of Kalibukbuk, primarily as a tourist attraction. However, in 1995 to commemorate the 50th anniversary of Indonesian Independence, the regional government decided to hold the event in its original form on a flooded ricefield in the village of Banjar, and plans to make this an annual event. The winner is not necessarily the fastest; the appearance of the bull and driver are an important consideration when the judge decides the overall winner.

Around Lovina

About 5 km to the west of Lovina there are waterfalls at the village of **Labuhan Haji**, and a Buddhist monastery near the village of **Banjar Tegeha**, nearby which there are **hot springs** ① *6000Rp adult, drivers will offer to take tourists there and back again for 150,000Rp, but this can easily be bargained down to 50,000Rp*. The cleanliness of some of the pools is dubious. Make sure you bathe in one that has a fast flow of water running into it. To the south there are cool highland areas with **lakes** and **botanical gardens** in the area surrounding Bedugul and Gunung Batur; it can be very wet here except at the height of the dry season. To the east is **Singaraja**, the capital of the district, and beyond Singaraja there are interesting temples and other cultural sites, and the *gamelan* village of **Sawan**.

East Bali, Karangasem and the north coast listings

For Sleeping and Eating price codes and other relevant information, see pages 7-10.

🛏 Sleeping

Tirtagangga *p72*

$$$$ Tirta Ayu, in the grounds of the water garden, T0363 22503, www.hotel tirtagangga.com. 4 comfortable a/c cottages with bathroom featuring sunken bath and shower with water spouting from a demonic head. Free access to the bathing pools in the water garden.

$ Dhangin Taman Inn, T0363 22059. With a garden overlooking the water gardens, this place has whacky bright tiling and psychedelic ponds. Cleanish rooms, fair value.

Amed *p72*

All accommodation is along the coastal road, and spread out over 11 km. The greatest concentration of places is from Jemeluk to Bunutan. Price codes reflect low season. Many places double their rates in high season; always negotiate as prices quoted are far too high. Most places have a restaurant but quality varies wildly.

$$$$ Apa Kabar Villas, T0363 23492, www.apakabarvillas.com. Beautifully decorated cottages with spacious bathrooms containing fish pond and bath, rooms here can accommodate up to 4 people. The hotel is next to the beach and has a pool, full spa service and a top-notch restaurant. Discounts available.

$$$ Anda Amed, T0363 23498, www. andaamedresort.com. This hotel injects a bit of glamour to Amed's lodging choices with contemporary design, a sleek pool and a Moorish terrace area. Online discounts available.

$$$ Puri Wisata Resort and Spa, T0363 23523, www.diveamed.com. Right down on the beach, the a/c rooms here are big, some with private terrace looking out on the sea. Some rooms are located in a block

at the back and have no view at all. There is a pool, dive centre (see Activities and tours, page 86) and full spa service.

$$$ Santai, T0363 23487, www.santaibali. com. The 10 thatched a/c cottages, with enough space to sleep 4, are tastefully decorated and have a verdant outdoor bathroom. The hotel has a pool, and is right on the beach. You can rent (expensive) bikes here.

$$$-$$ Waeni's, T0363 23515, www.bali waenis.com. Perched high on a headland, these cottages have stunning views of the sea and the surrounding hills; Gunung Agung can be seen clearly in the mornings, wrapped in cloud. The rooms are comfortable and have a great outdoors lounging area with bed and hammock. Service is friendly and the restaurant serves some great Balinese food. Recommended.

$$ Prema Liong, T0363 23486, www.bali-amed.com. The low-season prices for the 4 thatched cottages here are good value. Cottages are set in a lush garden on the hillside, and the sea can just about be seen through the foliage. They have spacious verandas with plenty of lounging potential. Average restaurant. Recommended.

$$ Wawa Wewe 2, T0363 23506, www.bali-wawawewe.com/en. On the beach, with a pool. Wide selection of rooms, including a well-furnished family room with space for 4 with sea view. Occasional performances of local dances and *gamelan* music. Book exchange. Restaurant serving excellent local and Western cuisine and play area for children.

Padangbai *p73, map p73*

The most attractive rooms are in town but the best location is to the north along the bay, where rooms and bungalows are surrounded by gardens and coconut groves and are quieter. You won't find the luxury of Ubud or Seminyak here, but there is a lot of simple, good-value accommodation.

$$$$-$$$ Bloo Lagoon, Jln Silayukti, T0363 41211, www.bloolagoon.com. Built on eco/green principles, this top-end joint is connected to the rest of town by a small paved road and offers gorgeous views from its cottages of the harbour or north towards Candidasa. Rooms are mostly fan cooled and a/c is chargeable in some rooms. Delicious daily breakfast and decent lap pool to work off any excess calories. Recommended.

$$ Mustika Sari Hotel, Jln Silayukti, T0363 21540. www.mustikasaribeach.com. The hotel is set in pleasant gardens and has a pool and massage service. Rooms are large, clean and have a/c, TV, and bathroom with a bath. Sizeable discounts available.

$$ Puri Rai, Jln Silayuktil 7, T0363 41385, www.puriraihotel.com. The 30 a/c and fan rooms here are spacious, and clean with TV and fridge. Pool. Good value in this price range.

$ Billabong, Jln Silayukti, T0363 41399. The free breakfasts are good, and the simple rattan-walled bungalows are acceptable, but not as good value as the standard bungalows, some of which have a sea view.

$ Pondok Serangan Inn, 2 Jln Silayukti, T0363 41425. Friendly and quiet place with spacious fan and a/c rooms with hot water. The communal veranda on the 2nd floor has great view over the rooftops of the town and the boats in the bay. Recommended.

$ Pondok Wisata Parta, Jln Silayukti, Gang Tongkol 7, T0363 41475. Next door to the Dharma, the rooms are of a similar standard, although the locks on the doors and windows could do with being replaced. You can just about see the sea through a gap in the buildings in front.

$ Topi Inn, Jln Silayukti 99, T0363 41424, www.topiinn.nl. The 5 rooms here are average and quite dark, and with the smaller ones, guests have to use a communal bathroom. Nevertheless there is a great common veranda with a hammock and cushions scattered around, and sea views, making this the most social place to stay in Padangbai. Breakfast is not included in the price. The larger rooms with attached bathroom are often full, so it might be worth reserving in advance.

Padangbai to Candi Dasa *p74*

$$$$ Alila Manggis, Buitan, T0363 41011, www.alilahotels.com/manggis. Luxury hotel with 54 stylish rooms looking out onto a delightful coconut grove, and the ocean beyond. The hotel employs stunning use of lighting, which creates a soothing effect in the evenings. Cooking and diving courses offered. Pool. Good discounts available for online booking.

$$$$ Amankila, outside Candi Dasa near the village of Manggis, T0363 41333, www. amanresorts.com. One of the renowned **Aman** group of hotels, in an outstanding location spread out over the hillside with stunning sea views. Designed with simple elegance to create a calming and peaceful milieu. With only 35 guest pavilions and 3 vast swimming pools on different levels of the hill, it is easy to imagine you are the only guest in residence.

$$$ Matahari Beach Bungalows, Buitan, Manggis, postal address: PO Box 287, Denpasar 80001, T0363 41008/41009. Signposted from the main road, follow a steep path down the hill for about 50 m. Beautiful secluded setting in a large coconut grove beside the sea, with a beach suitable for swimming though occasionally there is a current. 11 fairly attractive bungalows and rooms, very clean, some large family rooms, several of the cheapest rooms have a shared ceiling so your neighbours will probably hear your every movement. Ketut, the owner, speaks good English and is very helpful and knowledgeable about Bali.

$$ Ampel Bungalows, Manggis Beach, 6 km from Candi Dasa, just off the main road, T0363 41209. A peaceful, rural setting overlooking rice paddies and the sea. 4 simple, very clean bungalows, with private *mandi*, signposted from the main road shortly after the **Amankila Hotel**.

Candi Dasa *p74, map p74*

There are plenty of accommodation choices in Candi Dasa (almost too many), although as the number of tourists has fallen, the upkeep of many of the places seems to have declined. Still, there are some good bargains to be had, and some stunning sea views. Most of the accommodation is on the seaward side of Jln Raya Candi Dasa. At the eastern end of Candi Dasa, where the main road bends to the left, a small road (Jln Banjar Samuh) leads off on the right, lined with accommodation on the seaward side. Known as **Samuh village**, this slightly rural area is perhaps the most attractive place to stay. Most places include breakfast in their rates. Most hotels with swimming pools allow non-residents to use their pools for a small charge.

$$$$ Villa Sassoon, Jln Puri Bagus, T0363 41511, www.villasasoon.com. Perfect for those seeking a little romance, the spacious, private villa compounds have 2 en suite cottages and a further cottage with living room and kitchen area. The buildings face a central pool and outdoor lounging area. It's all very sleek and modern. Good discounts available for stays of more than 7 days.

$$$$-$$$ The Watergarden, Jln Raya Candi Dasa, T0363 41540, www.water gardenhotel.com. The beautiful, lush tropical gardens are filled with a variety of water features, and the private cottages have koi-filled lily ponds around the veranda. Rooms are spacious, spotless and quiet. There are good mountain views between the abundant foliage. This place is popular with foreign couples seeking a Balinese-style wedding. Pool, bar. Recommended. Discounts available.

$$$ Alam Asmara, Jln Raya Candi Dasa, T0363 41929, www.alamasmara.com. Small fish-filled streams line the pathways in this new resort that offers elegant cottages with high ceilings and outdoor

bathroom. Bedrooms have a safe and TV (no international channels). There is a resident Dive Master and a variety of diving courses are offered. Pool, access to the sea and full spa service. Discounts available.

$$$-$$ The Grand Natia Bungalows, Jln Raya Candi Dasa, T0363 42007, www.indo.com/hotels/grand_natia. A path lined on both sides with koi-filled streams surrounds the 12 a/c cottages. The more expensive cottages have sea views from outside, but not from the bedrooms themselves. Cottages are tastefully decorated, and have a fridge. Pool.

$$$-$ Puri Oka, Jln Puri Bagus, T0363 41092. Large selection of rooms, some of which are vastly better value than the others. Cheap fan rooms are clean but have no hot water. Some of the a/c rooms need to be redecorated, but others, such as the sea-view rooms, feature TV, DVD player, outdoor bathroom and are tastefully decorated. The star is the spacious suite on the 2nd floor with plenty of light and a private terrace overlooking the sea. Pool.

$$ Dasa Wana, Jln Raya Candi Dasa, T0363 41444. Variety of bungalows, with living room, kitchen and bathroom with bath. Some bungalows are much better furnished than others, so ask to see a selection. This place is not on the seaward side of the main road, but has great views of the mountains behind. Pool.

$$ Geringsering, Jln Raya Candi Dasa, T0363 41084. The 4 a/c rooms here are huge, 2 of which have lovely sea views and are filled with the sound of the surf. Room have mosquito nets. Tax not included in the price.

$$ Ida's Homestay, Jln Raya Candi Dasa, T0363 41096, jsidas@aol.com. An anomaly in Candi Dasa's accommodation choice in that it is set in a spacious palm grove, with the cottages being a minor feature of the property. Ida Ayu Srihati, the owner, has an extensive collection of Indonesian antiques that can be found littering the grounds; there's even an entire rice barn from

Madura transplanted here. The gardens lead down to a small beach and a decking area overlooking the sea. There are 5 simple fan cottages, which are often full. Things are kept rustic, with a cow wandering the grove, chickens running free and hot water provided on demand rather than on tap. Book in advance. Recommended.

$$-$ Iguana Bungalows, Jln Raya Candi Dasa, T0363 41973, iguana_cafe_bali@ yahoo.com. The dense tropical garden contains a/c and fan bungalows that are clean, but look slightly worn, particularly the bathrooms. Some rooms have great sea views. Pool.

$$-$ Seaside Cottages, Jln Raya Candi Dasa, T0363 41629, www.balibeachfront-cottages.com. Set in pleasant tropical gardens leading down to the sea, with a good selection of bungalows. The small fan rooms have a single bed, but are clean and have attached bathroom. The larger bungalows have a/c and some have wonderful sea views. Tax and breakfast are not included in the price. Massage and salon services available.

$ Agung Bungalows, Jln Raya Candi Dasa, T0363 41535. Cheap, clean fan-only rattan-walled bungalows, some have excellent sea views (ask for the rooms at the front of the property). There's an enticing strip of beach here. Recommended.

Sengkidu village *p76*

$$$ Candi Beach Cottage, reservations: PO Box 3308, Denpasar 80033, T0363 41234, www.candibeachbali.com. Luxury hotel set in large, scenic tropical gardens, in a quiet location beside sea with access to beach, offering everything you would expect from a hotel in this class, popular with tour groups.

$$ Dwi Utama, T0363 41053. Offers 6 very clean rooms, with fan, private bathroom, beachside restaurant (cheap), access to good, small beach, well-tended, small garden, peaceful, good value.

$$ Nusa Indah Bungalows, Sengkidu, signposted and reached via a separate track to the left of the temple. Set in a peaceful location beside the sea, amid coconut groves and rice paddies, 7 clean, simple bungalows with fan, access to small, rocky beach, beachside restaurant (**$**).

$$ Pondok Bananas (Pisang), T0363 41065. Family-run, 4 spotless rooms. Bungalows set in a large coconut grove beside the sea with access to beach, very peaceful and secluded.

$$ Puri Amarta (Amarta Beach Bungalows), T0363 41230. 10 bungalows set in large, attractive gardens beside the sea and beach, well run and very popular, liable to be full even off season, restaurant (**$**) beside sea.

Lovina *p76, map p77*

Mosquitoes can be a problem, not all bungalows provide nets. The central area of Kalibukbuk has the greatest concentration of accommodation, the widest choice of restaurants and nightlife, and most of the tourist facilities; however, it is becoming built up. Some of the side roads to the east in the Anturan area offer more attractive and peaceful surroundings.

Kalibukbuk

$$-$ Bayu Kartika Beach Resort, Jln Ketapang, T0362 41055, www.bayukartika resort.com. Lots of space in this 2-ha resort and featuring (so the owner claims) the largest pool in Lovina. Many rooms face the sea, but are a little faded. The more expensive rooms have an open-air bathroom. Interestingly, there is a monitor lizard pond. Popular.

$$-$ Nirwana Seaside Cottages, Jln Bina Ria, T0362 41288, www.nirwanaseaside.com. Set in huge, pleasant gardens, this hotel has a range of a/c and fan rooms, some with sea view. The clean de luxe rooms, feature bath and a pleasant veranda, but the 2-storey bungalows with fan represent better value and come with a sea view. Pool.

$$-$ Puri Bali Cottages, Jln Ketapang, T0362 41485, www.puribalilovina.com. Selection of a/c and fan rooms in a garden. Rooms are large and have hot water, but are a little decrepit. Cheaper ones come with a mosquito net. Pool and basketball area for those who fancy shooting some hoops under the tropical sun.

$$-$ Rini, Jln Ketapang, T0362 41386, www.rinihotel.homepage.dk. In a large compound with a saltwater swimming pool, this hotel has an excellent selection of well-designed a/c and fan rooms, some of which are cavernous, with equally large balconies. The largest rooms are the upstairs fan rooms in the 2-storey buildings and have nice sunset views. Friendly staff. Recommended.

$$-$ Villa Jaya, Jln Ketapang, T0362 700 1238. 100 m down a path off Jln Ketapang. New hotel with cosy fan and a/c rooms. Pool and views of the surrounding rice fields.

Banyualit

This area is much quieter, but offers the usual range of facilities, including internet cafés, cheap restaurants and provision stores.

$$$ Banyualit Spa and Resort, Jln Banyualit, T0362 41789, www.banyualit. com. Range of rooms set in a lush garden. A/c rooms are clean and have TV, but are a little cramped and dark. The fan rooms, with rattan walls are very simple and hugely overpriced. Full spa service with a host of friendly staff. Pool.

$$-$ Suma, Jln Banyualit, T0362 41566, www.sumahotel.com. The staff are very welcoming at this hotel with clean and comfortable a/c and fan rooms. Pool and spa.

$ Ray Beach Inn, Jln Banyualit, T0362 41088. Cheap, clean fan rooms and spa service.

Beachfront

$$$$-$$$ Sunari (formerly Sol Lovina), Jln Raya Lovina, T0362 41775, www.sunari.com. A full range of facilities is available in this hotel including spa and gym. Rooms are spacious and the more expensive have private garden and a plunge pool. Business doesn't seem too brisk here. 50% discounts available.

$$$ Aneka, Jln Raya Lovina, T0362 41121, www.aneka-lovina.com. This popular resort has 59 a/c rooms that are clean, well decorated and comfortable. The resort has a pool near the beach, fitness centre and offers Balinese dance lessons. Discounts available.

🍴 Eating

Tirtagangga *p72*

There are a few choices, mainly around the water garden.

$$ Tirta Ayu, (see Sleeping) is the best restaurant here, with sublime views and serving fair international cuisine.

$ Gangga Café, T0363 22041. Open 0700-2200. Cheap eatery near the entrance to the gardens, serves delicious home-made yoghurt, curries and Balinese food.

Amed *p72*

Many people choose to eat in the restaurants attached to their hotel. However, there are a handful of eateries along the road.

$$ Pazzo, T0828 368 5498. Open 1000-2300. Pasta, pizza and the usual Western fare alongside a fair selection of Indonesian dishes. **Pazzo** doubles as a popular bar with a choice of wines and cocktails, live music, pool and Balinese dancing.

$$ Wawa Wewe 1, 400 m down the road (away from Amed) from the hotel of the same name, T0363 23506. Open 0800-2200. This friendly restaurant has a good selection of international food and Balinese cuisine.

$ Ari's Warung, T0852 3788 2015, open 0900-2100, and **Café C'est Bon**, T0852 3482 66778, open 0900-2200. Both these small places look a little forlorn with a distinct lack of custom. This is a shame as they are both good places to try the catch of the day with tasty Balinese sauces. Both have sea views, and **Ari's Warung** offers free transport to and from the restaurant.

Padangbai *p73, map p73*

When you're a limp stone's throw to the sea, the seafood is going to be good, as is the case in Padangbai. It is quite common to see women walking around with large freshly caught yellow fin tuna thrown over their shoulder. Many of the hotels have restaurants, and there are numerous restaurants along the shoreline serving up the usual Indonesian and Western dishes. There are a lot of cheap *warungs* around the port and on Jln Pelabuhan Padangbai.

$$ Topi Inn (see Sleeping). Open 0730-2300. The best place to eat in Padangbai, with an extensive menu of fresh seafood, vegetarian dishes, great salads and delights such as a delicious cheese platter with olives. The staff are friendly and the restaurant is deservedly popular. You can refill your used water bottle here with fresh drinking water for 1000Rp.

$ Café Papa John, Jln Segara. Open 0700-2200. Good spot to watch the world go by and see boats pulling in to the bay. The delicious fish kebabs are served in a tangy spicy sauce.

$ Depot Segara, Jln Segara, T0363 41443. Open 0800-2200. Friendly staff and an acoustic guitar propped up the in the corner point to good times at this relaxed eatery offering a range of Balinese food and fresh seafood. The fish *sate* is super and freshly made each morning. There is also the usual range of sandwiches, burgers and good chilled lassis.

Candi Dasa *p74, map p74*

There are a variety of well-priced restaurants dotted along the main road with similar menus; seafood is the best bet. Most restaurants cater to perceived European tastes, which can be disappointing for anyone who likes Indonesian food. Many of the hotels have restaurants, often with sea views. The following are also recommended

though quality and ingredients can vary enormously from day to day; you might have a delicious meal one day, order the exact same dish the next day and be disappointed.

$$ Candi Dasa Café, Jln Raya Candi Dasa, T0363 41107. Open 0800-2300. Clean and comfortable restaurant, Balinese fare and *rijstafel*. Delicious icy ginger ale.

$$ Ganesha, Jln Raya Candi Dasa, T0813 3811 2898. Good-value set meals, plenty of fresh seafood, and suckling pig at this friendly good-value eatery, which has *legong* and mask dance performances nightly at 1930.

$$ Kubu Bali, Jln Raya Candi Dasa, T0363 41532. Specializes in seafood with fish, lobster and crab dishes cooked a variety of ways. Some standard international dishes.

$$ Toke, Jln Raya Candi Dasa, T0363 41991. Open 1100-2300. Known for its Indian cuisine, this is the place in Candi Dasa to get good mushroom *masala*, *naan* and *aloo gobi*. There's an extensive list of cocktails, and an excellent range of Western food. The kitchen here is open, so diners can watch their dinner being prepared. Recommended.

$$ The Watergarden, Jln Raya Candi Dasa, T0363 41540. Open 0700-2300. Excellent array of fresh seafood, including delicious *ikan pepes* and grilled *mahi mahi* glazed with soy sauce, available in this peaceful setting of lily ponds and fountains. Also international favourites and plenty of salads, as well as Dom Pérignon champagne for those in the mood to really push the boat out. Good service. Recommended.

$ Raja's, Jln Raya Candi Dasa, T0363 42034. Open 0800-2200. This well-established roadside restaurant with pool table and an extensive selection of DVDs, has a good menu of set meals, including an Indian menu offering Goan curries and an interesting pork and banana curry. Happy hour 1700-1900.

$ Srijati, Jln Raya Candi Dasa. Open 0700-2100. Rustic and cheap venue to grab a lunch of *nasi goreng* or *opor ayam*. Also a fair number of authentic Balinese dishes.

Lovina *p76, map p77*

Lovina offers a great chance to tuck into some good, fresh seafood with excellent Balinese sauces, although there are plenty of places serving reasonable Western fare. There is also a line of *kaki-lima* and small *warungs* selling cheap *bakso*, *nasi goreng*, *roti bakar* and some Balinese street food on Jln Raya Lovina, near the traffic lights at the end of Jln Ketupang. It opens when the sun sets.

$$ Bali Apik, Jln Bina Ria, T0362 41050. Open 0800-2300. Slow staff, but a good range of vegetarian dishes and a good seafood menu that includes tasty tuna fish *sate*.

$$ Barcelona, Jln Ketupang, T0362 41894. Open 0900-2300. Popular family-run place, one of the better places to try Balinese food in Lovina. The *pepes babi guling* (grilled pork cooked in a banana leaf) and *sate pelecing* (fish *sate* with Balinese sauce) are excellent.

$$ Jasmine Kitchen, Jln Bina Ria, T0362 41565, jasminekitchen@beeb.net. Open 1130-2230. The cheery owner serves up good Thai favourites such as tom yum soup, steamed fish in a lime, lemongrass and coriander dressing and some delicious home-made cakes to the sound of the sitar in a relaxed setting. The specials are worth investigating.

$$ Kakatua, Jln Bina Ria, T0362 41144. Open 0800-2300. The water features make this restaurant a mellow place, serving Burmese fishballs, home-made cakes and baked fish.

$ Bakery Lovina, Jln Raya Lovina, T0362 42225. Open 0730-2130. This mini-market selling a range of cheeses, meats, wines and tinned Western food for the local expat community also makes excellent sandwiches, fresh bread and cakes.

$ Khi Khi, Jln Raya Lovina, T0362 41548. Open 1000-2200. Excellent-value seafood sets that allow a choice of fish, Balinese *bumbu* (dressing) a Chinese-style sauce, and a large bowl of rice. The restaurant is simple and unfussy and has an open kitchen.

$ Spunky's, on the beach near the Aneka Hotel, T0813 373 6509. Open 1300-2400. Owned by an Englishman, this is the place for homesick British tourists to get a long overdue helping of ham or sausage and egg. Also daily seafood specials. An unbeatable location – select one of the many cocktails on offer and watch the sun go down.

Bars and clubs

Padangbai *p73, map p73*
Babylon Bar and Kinky Reggae Bar on Jln Silyakuti open in the afternoon and serve booze until late.

Zen Inn, Jln Segara, T0819 3309 2012. Open 0700-2300. Serves pies with mash and gravy, and rocks until almost 2400 with live music and a video screen in a comfortable and friendly pub-like setting.

Lovina *p76, map p77*
Many of the places on Jln Bina Ria offer all-day happy hour in an attempt to lure customers, but don't expect sophisticated nightlife. Head to ZiGiZ Bar on Jln Bina Ria for live acoustic music, cocktails and cable TV showing live sporting events.

Entertainment

Candi Dasa *p74, map p74*
Balinese dance performances are staged nightly at various restaurants in town, though are nowhere near Ubud quality.

Shopping

Semarapura and around *p71*
Textiles Although good examples are hard to find, Semarapura is the centre of the production of royal *songket* cloth, traditionally silk but today more often synthetic. The cloth is worn for ceremonial occasions and characteristically features floral designs, geometric patterns, *wayang* figures and animals. It takes 2 months to weave a good piece.

Padangbai *p73, map p73*
Books Wayan's Bookstore, Jln Penataran Agung, T0819 1615 3587. Open 0800-1800. On the way up to Pantai Cecil, down a small lane on the right-hand side. Huge sign on the roof in red letters. Has the best selection of second-hand books in Padangbai. Also offers rental and exchange services.

Candi Dasa *p74, map p74*
Books The best place is the Candi Dasa Bookstore, which has a reasonable selection of books on Bali and Indonesia as well as second-hand books, magazines and newspapers. The lady who runs it speaks excellent English.

Crafts Geringsing, Jln Raya Candi Dasa, T0363 41084, open 0900-1800, sells double *ikat* cloth from Tenganan and other Balinese arts and crafts. **Lenia**, Jln Raya Candi Dasa T0363 41759, open 1000-2000, a good place to see *ata* baskets, which are made from a locally grown vine much more durable than rattan. Water resistant, it is claimed these baskets can last for up to 100 years. There is also a small selection of Sumba blankets and other quality crafts. **Nusantara**, Jln Raya Candi Dasa, open 0900-2100, is also a good place to pick up locally made handicrafts.

Groceries Asri, fixed-price store for film, food and medicine.

Tailor The lady who runs the Candi Dasa Bookstore is also a tailor.

▲▲ Activities and tours

Amed *p72*
Body and soul
A Spa, T0813 3823 8846, open 1000-1900. Lots on offer, including an Indonesian massage, US$18 for 1 hr, and a 90-min calming back treatment, US$26. Roaming masseuses pop into hotels throughout the day clutching comments from satisfied customers looking for business. Bargain hard.

Diving and snorkelling
The reef in Amed is very close to the beach, and the resorts are not far from the *USAT Liberty* wreck at Tulamben. Snorkelling gear can be hired from hotels or stalls along the road for between 30,000Rp and 40,000Rp per day. **ECO Dive Bali**, T0363 23482, www.ecodive bali.com. Offers dives at Tulamben (US$95 for 2 dives), and in locations in Amed. Also runs a variety of courses including the Open Water course for US$375. **Puri Wirata Dive Centre**, T0363 23523. Slightly cheaper; for dives at Tulamben, at the nearby Japanese wreck. Open Water course also offered.

Padangbai *p73, map p73*
Diving and snorkelling
Diving is a popular activity in Padangbai, with numerous operators along Jln Silayukti. Dives can be taken in waters around Padangbai, at nearby **Gili Biaha** with its shark cave, and further afield at the wreck of the *USAT Liberty Bell* at Tulamben. Marine life that can be seen includes the giant tuna, napoleon wrasse, sea turtles and sharks. You can pick up a snorkel set along the seafront for 30,000Rp (though you'll have to bargain) and find reasonable snorkelling at the **Blue Lagoon Beach** over the headland at the east end of the town. **Geko Dive**, Jln Silayukti, T0363 41516, www.gekodive.com. This professional company offers PADI Open Water courses for US$400, Rescue Diver for US$350. Also runs a Discover Scuba session for diving novices in their pool for US$75. **OK Divers**, Jln Silayukti, T0363 41790, www.divingbali.cz. A popular Czech outfit that offers 2 dives for US$70, the PADI Open Water course for US$470, and Rescue Diver for US$470.

Workshops

Topi Inn (see Sleeping) has workshops on a wide variety of topics including Balinese woodcarving, coconut tree climbing, batik and *ikat* weaving. You can also join discussions on Balinese Hinduism.

Candi Dasa *p74, map p74*
Diving and snorkelling

Boat hire and snorkelling trips to Nusa Lembongan (US$40) can be organized through **Beli Made Tam**, T0818 551752, on the beach near the Puri Bali Hotel. He also offers snorkelling trips to White Sand Beach (3 hrs including equipment US$35). You can rent snorkelling equipment from him for 30,000Rp for 2 hrs.

Sub Ocean Bali, Jln Raya Candi Dasa, T0363 41411, www.suboceanbali.com. 5-star PADI dive centre offering trips to Nusa Penida, Tulamben and Gili Mimpang. They also rent snorkelling equipment

Lovina *p76, map p77*
Boats and fishing

Tours are organized by the larger hotels, tour and dive companies and *losmen* for 75,000Rp an hr per person. The wonderfully named **Captain Ketut Bonanza** (T0813 3822 1175) has excellent English and can regale customers with tales of tiger sharks and sea snakes.

Body and soul

Araminth Spa, Jln Ketapang, T0362 41901. Open 0900-1900. Variety of treatments available including facials (US$9.20), ayurvedic massage (US$25) and Indonesian treatments such *as mandi lulur* and *mandi rempah* (spice bath).

Bali Samadhi Spa, Jln Ketapang, T08133 855 8260, www.bali samadhi.com. Open 0900-1800. Similar to Araminth Spa.

Cooking

Putu's Home Cooking, T08122 856 3705. Includes a trip to the local market and instruction in cooking 7 Balinese dishes

followed by a local feast. Lesson lasts 4-5 hrs, US$20 per person.

Diving and snorkelling

Average snorkelling just off the beach. Snorkel hire 20,000Rp for 1 hr or 100,000Rp an hr with a boat and captain; better marine life at Menjangan Island (with Spice Dive, below). Equipment available from boat owners and dive shops, not all of equal quality.

Spice Dive, Jln Bina Ria, T0362 41305, www.balispicedive.com. The waters around Lovina are not particularly special for diving, so this highly regarded dive centre offers a variety of diving courses and trips to nearby diving locations such as Pulau Menjangan and Tulamben as well as Zen Beach for muck diving. Introduction dives cost US$60, and a PADI Open Water course costs US$350. Rescue Diver, Dive Master and many other courses are also offered.

Swimming and watersports

Most big hotels will let non-residents use the pool for between 10,000Rp and 20,000Rp if you look presentable.
Spunky's, on the beach in Banyualit (see Eating). Rents jet skis for US$70 per hr, surf bikes for US$10 per hr, canoes for US$5 per hr, and catamarans for US$20 per hr.

Trekking

Trekking in the area around Sambangan village can be organized through **Putu Puspa**, T0815 5857 7404 and includes walks through rice fields, and waterfalls and visits to meditation caves for US$15 (short trek) to US$30 for a longer trek.

⊖ Transport

Semarapura and around *p71*
Bemo

Connections with **Denpasar**'s Batubulan terminal and points east – **Besakih**, **Amlapura**, **Candi Dasa**.

Boat

Kusamba, from where there are boats to **Nusa Penida**.

Tirtagangga *p72*
Bemo

Connect Tirtagangga with **Semarapura** and **Singaraja** (for connections with Lovina).

Shuttle

2 daily to/from **Padangbai**, US$12.50.

Amed *p72*
Bemo

From **Semarapura** catch a bemo heading north to **Culik** (22,000Rp) and **Singaraja**. Change bemos at Culik; until 1200 there are a limited number of bright red bemos running along the coast east to **Amed** and **Lipah**, after 1200 you can catch an ojek or try and hitch a lift, otherwise it is a long walk.

Car

45 mins from **Candi Dasa**.

Padangbai *p73, map p73*
Bemo

Padangbai is 2.5 km off the main coastal road; connections with **Denpasar**'s Batubulan terminal, **Candi Dasa** and **Amlapura**. Blue bemos run to **Semarapura**, 18,000Rp, and orange bemos run to **Amlapura**, 18,000Rp.

Boat

Ferries for Lembar on **Lombok** leave around the clock daily, every 1½ hrs, and take 4-5 hrs depending on the seas, 35,000Rp adult, 22,000Rp child, adult plus motorbike 92,000Rp (includes 1 or 2 passengers). The busiest departure is 0800, which is fine if one of the 2 large fairly modern ferries is doing that sailing; otherwise try to get on as early as possible to secure a decent seat. To the **Gili Islands**, the fastest way is using **Gili Cat** (Padangbai agent: Jln Silayukti, T0363 41441, www.gilicat.com). Their boats leave Padangbai

daily at 1130 and sail to **Gili Trawangan** in 1½ hrs, US$66 one-way, US$120 for a return. Equally direct, but taking longer is the **Perama** boat, which leaves Padangbai at 1330 and arrives on Gili Trawangan 4 hrs later, US$30. Aggressive porters at the ferry terminal can be a real pain. They try and grab your luggage, carry it on board and then charge an outrageous amount. If you need help to carry your belongings, negotiate a fair price beforehand. 10000Rp per piece should cover it.

Bus

From the bus station you can catch long-distance buses, west to **Java** and east to **Sumbawa** and **Lombok**.

Shuttle

Perama office: Jln Pelabuhan Padangbai, T0363 41419. Daily connections to **Kuta** and **Ngurah Rai Airport**, 3 daily, US$6, **Ubud**, 3 daily, US$5, **Candi Dasa**, 3 daily, US$2.50 (sometimes the **Perama** shuttle to Candi Dasa does not run due to lack of customers and it will be necessary to jump on the orange bemo to Amlapura, 18,000Rp or hire a bemo, US$6). To **Lovina**, 1 daily (via Ubud), US$15, **Senggigi**, 2 daily, US$10 and **Mataram**, 2 daily, US$10.

Candi Dasa *p74, map p74*
Bemo

Regular connections with **Denpasar**'s Batubulan terminal (2 hrs 10 mins), **Amlapura** and **Semarapura**.

Bicycle hire

From **Srijati** (see Eating) for 20,000Rp a day.

Car/motorcycle hire

From hotels, *losmen* and from shops along the main road.

Shuttle

Can be found at the western end of Jln Raya Candi Dasa, T0363 41114. To **Kuta** and **Ngurah Rai Airport**, 3 daily, US$6. **Ubud**,

3 daily, US$5. **Lovina**, 1 daily, US$15 via Ubud. **Padangbai**, 3 daily, US$2.50. Also to **Amed**, 2 daily, US$12.50, 2 people minimum. It's just as easy to hire an ojek for the ride costing around US$10, including a stop in **Tirtagangga** (30 mins). If you want to go to Lombok, they will shuttle you first to the office in Padangbai.

Lovina *p76, map p77*
Bus
From **Denpasar**'s Ubung terminal, catch an express bus to **Singaraja**, 1½-2 hrs, from where there are regular buses to Lovina. There are also regular buses and minibuses from **Gilimanuk**, taking the north coast route, 1½ hrs (buses from Java will drop passengers off at Gilimanuk to catch a connection to Lovina – sometimes included in the cost of the ferry and bus ticket). Buses to Gilimanuk for the ferry to Java cost US$3. To **Java** jump on a Singaraja–Java bus as it passes along Jln Raya Lovina. Tickets need to be booked a day in advance and can be bought in several places in Kalibukbuk. To **Jakarta**, US$35, to **Yogyakarta**, US$27, **Surabaya**, US$14, and **Probolinggo** (for Gunung Bromo) is US$13.

Car/motorbike/bicycle hire
From several places around town for US$11/US$4/US$2 per day.

Shuttle
Perama shuttles to **Kuta**, 1 daily, US$10. To **Ubud**, 1 daily, US$10. To **Padangbai**, 1 daily, US$15. To **Candi Dasa**, 1 daily, US$15. Look around town for other shuttle bus prices, as Lovina is the one place **Perama** doesn't seem to have the monopoly; on arrival in Lovina, **Perama** takes passengers to their office in Anturan for a lunch of *nasi goreng*, while touts hover around offering accommodation. After beating off the touts, you get back on the **Perama** bus and are taken to your hotel.

❻ Directory

Semarapura and around *p71*
Post office To the west of the Kherta Ghosa.

Padangbai *p73, map p73*
Banks Money changers along Jln Segara and Jln Silayukti. **Immigration** Jln Penataran Agung. **Internet** The connection isn't particularly good, and sometimes there is no access. Try the Gili Cat office (see Transport). **Police** Jln Pelabuhan Padangbai, T0363 41388.

Candi Dasa *p74, map p74*
Banks There are plenty of money changers along Jln Raya Candi Dasa, although rates are variable. **Internet** Jln Raya Candi Dasa.

Lovina *p76, map p77*
Banks On the main road. There is a BCA ATM on Jln Raya Lovina. **Internet** The most popular place is Bitsandbites, Jln Raya Lovina, T0362 41430, open 1000-2200, 15,000Rp per hr. **Medical services** Pharmacy, Jln Raya.

West coast Lombok

Senggigi Beach stretches over 8 km from Batulayar to Mangsit. The road from Mataram to Bangsal winds through impressive tropical forest in the foothills of Mount Rinjani. Travelling further north along the coast from Mangsit, the road reaches Bangsal, the 'port' for boats to the Gilis. Senggigi is the most developed tourist area on Lombok, with a range of hotels. The beaches here – and they extend over several kilometres – are picturesque and the backdrop of mountains and fabulous sunsets adds to the ambience.

The Gili Islands are becoming increasingly expensive and are no longer primarily geared to backpackers. There are no vehicles and there really isn't much more to do beyond sunbathing, swimming, snorkelling, walking, drinking and generally relaxing.

Senggigi → *For listings, see pages 94-96. Phone code: 0370.*

Senggigi lies 12 km north of Mataram on the west coast. The beach overlooks the famous Lombok Strait, which the English naturalist Alfred Russel Wallace postulated divided the Asian and Australasian zoological realms. The sacred Mount Agung on Bali can usually be seen shimmering in the distance. While Senggigi village supports the main concentration of shops, bars, restaurants and tour companies, hotels and bungalows stretch along the coast and the road for several kilometres, from **Batulayar Beach** in the south, to **Batubolong**, **Senggigi** and **Mangsit** beaches to the north. Mangsit is quieter and less developed.

Many visitors express disappointment with Senggigi Beach itself, which is rather tatty and not very attractive. The town's downfall as a destination has been meteoric. It never reached the status of Bali's main resorts and instead plunged dramatically in the wake of the Bali bombings: pavements are overgrown, rubbish lies strewn about, businesses are shutting at an alarming rate and hotels lie derelict. The increasingly easy connections with the Gili islands from Bali mean that fewer and fewer tourists ever make it to the mainland. Senggigi has many hotels catering largely for the package tour trade, and they are not always particularly well managed or maintained. Their rates are highly negotiable off season. Many of the best guesthouses on Lombok are Balinese owned, and as prices on Bali rise inexorably, they no longer seem as overpriced as they once did.

Further north, this area becomes more beautiful and peaceful, with unspoilt, windswept beaches and lovely views across the Lombok Strait to Mount Agung on Bali and superb sunsets. They are currently free of the hawkers that so mar a visit to Senggigi itself.

Sights
About 2 km south of Senggigi, on a headland, is the **Batubolong Temple**. Unremarkable artistically (particularly when compared with the temples of Bali), it is named after a rock

with a hole in it (*Batu Bolong* or 'Hollow Rock') found here. Tourists come to watch the sun set over Bali; devotees come to watch it set over the sacred Mount Agung.

Each evening an informal **beach market** sets up on the beach in front of the **Senggigi Beach Hotel**; vendors lay out their wares: textiles, T-shirts, woodcarvings and 'antiques'. Heavy bargaining is required – these people really know how to sell.

Tours: Lombok to Flores via Komodo by boat

Indonesian life is inextricably linked with the vast amount of water that surrounds the myriad islands, and it is definitely worth spending some time on a boat while you're in the country. There are a couple of companies that offer boat trips from Lombok to **Labuanbajo** (Flores) via **Komodo Island**. The tours usually sail across the top of Sumbawa, stopping at Pulau Satonda for some snorkelling before continuing to Komodo and finally the port of Labuanbajo (Flores). Most trips last three days and two nights, and it is undoubtedly one of the most convenient ways of seeing the Komodo dragon. For many, is the highlight of a trip to Indonesia. It is wonderful to fall asleep on deck to the sound of the sea and wake up with the sunrise, gliding past desolate islands and distant coastlines. However, these boats can get packed with tourists, and as the old adage goes, a boat gets smaller each day you spend on it. The seas in this area can be highly unpredictable, and sailing in a seaworthy vessel in crucial. It makes sense to research the trip you wish to undertake thoroughly, and if the boat is going to be packed with other tourists, will the trip be enjoyable? **Perama** offers three-day/two-night trips starting at US$200 for a place on the deck, and US$260 for a cabin room. All meals are provided, though don't expect too much. (The first meal on board is usually quite lavish, but they go quickly downhill from there – stock up on crackers and snacks.) The trip to Labuanbajo departs every six days. The return trip from Labuanbajo takes lasts two days and one night and sails via **Rinca**, another place to see Komodo dragons, and costs US$130 for deck and US$180 for a cabin. There are plenty of good snorkelling stops on the tour. Both trips can be combined for a five-day/four-night epic, where both Komodo and Rinca are visited costing US$300 for deck class and US$400 for a cabin.

Bangsal → *For listings, see pages 94-96. Phone code: 0370.*

The coast road north from Senggigi is slow, steeply switchbacking over headlands and past some attractive beaches and a colony of monkeys. There is some surf on this part of the coast, mainly reef breaks, surfed by the locals on wooden boards.

Bangsal is just off the main road from Pemenang, and is little more than a tiny fishing village. However, as it is also the departure point for the Gilis, there are a couple of restaurants here that double up as tourist information centres, a ferry booking office, a money changer and a diving company. Vehicles stop around 300 m short of the harbour, and it is necessary to walk or charter a cidomo (7000Rp) to the ticket office. The harbour area is a tatty little place, full of scam artists who will surround travellers and try numerous tricks to extract money. These guys are a real headache. Ignore them, and head to the ticket office to buy your ticket to the island of your choice. Boats leave when they are full, and there is an announcement telling passengers when their boat is ready to depart. Boats to Gili Trawangan fill up the quickest, followed by boats to Gili Air, which has a large local population. Boats to Gili Meno can take some time to fill up. The fare to Gili Trawangan is 10000Rp, Gili Meno 9000Rp and Gili Air 8000Rp. Those that don't want to wait around can charter a boat at for around 185,000Rp to Gili Tranwangan, 165,000Rp to Gili Meno and 145,000Rp to Gili Air.

West coast Lombok listings

For Sleeping and Eating price codes and other relevant information, see pages 7-10.

😴 Sleeping

Senggigi *p92*

All the hotels and guesthouses are easily accessible by bemo from Mataram. The better hotels have generators for when the mains power fails, which it does quite often. Many of the cheaper hotels in Senggigi are poorly maintained, but the hotels in Batu Balong, 1 km from the centre are well-managed and popular and have access to a decent stretch of beach.

$$$$ Senggigi Beach Hotel, Jln Pantai Senggigi, T0370 693210, www.senggigi beach.aerowisata.com. Set in 12 ha of gardens, with tennis courts, spa, a huge chess board, and numerous bars and restaurants. Rooms are in comfortable a/c cottages with cable TV. The more expensive bungalows have a sea view.

$$$ Mascot Beach Resort, Jln Raya Senggigi, T0370 693365, mascot@telkom. net. Large selection of cottages in a large beachfront garden. More expensive ones have sea view. Rooms are simple and clean, and the more money you spend, the more space you get (and a bath thrown in). Discounts available. Recommended.

$$$ Sunset Cottages, Jln Raya Senggigi, T0370 692020, www.sunsethouse-lombok. com. 4 spacious rooms set in a block in a large garden, this place has effusive staff and access to the beach for splendid sunset views over the strait to Bali. Rooms are large and spotless, with cable TV and a veranda with sea view. Recommended.

$$$ Windy Beach Cottages, Mangsit, T0370 693191, www.windybeach.com. 14 attractive traditional-style thatched bungalows with fan and newly renovated private bathroom with shower/bath. Set in large gardens with an infinity pool amidst a coconut grove beside the sea, restaurant

($) offering good Indonesian, Chinese and Western food and a bar perfect for sunset drinks. Well managed. Recommended.

$$ Batu Bolong Cottages, Jln Raya Senggigi, T0370 693198. Well-managed hotel with a wide selection of cottages that straddle the busy road. Cheaper fan rooms have TV and are spacious and comfortable with a veranda facing the attractive garden. Somewhat tatty bathrooms. More expensive rooms have a/c and are closer to the beach.

$$ The Beach Club, Jln Raya Senggigi, T0370 693637, www.thebeachclublombok. com. Well-furnished a/c rooms with semi-open bathroom and veranda overlooking the beach. Cheaper backpacker rooms available, with communal area with TV and DVD player. Pool, popular bar, happy hour 1700-1900. One of Senggigi's better choices in this range. Recommended.

$$ Café Wayan, Jln Raya Senggigi, T0370 693098, www.alamindahbali.com. This Balinese-owned place has 4 spacious rooms with bathroom with bath. The ambience is laid-back and friendly.

🍴 Eating

Senggigi *p92*

There are not many independent restaurants on Senggigi – most eating places are attached to hotels. Independent restaurants are struggling. Many places offer free transport.

$$ Café Alberto, Jln Raya Senggigi, T0370 693039. Open 0900-2400. Good Italian food served on the seafront. Pizzas, pastas and seafood dishes dominate the menu. The cocktail list is extensive, and the view makes this an ideal spot for a sunset drink. They have a van that cruises the streets in the evening offering to drive people to the restaurant.

$$ Café Bumbu, Jln Raya Senggigi, T0370 692236. Open 0900-2300. Friendly. Offers fine Thai curries and salads, and has a great selection of Asian food, with some excellent deserts. Recommended.

$$ Square, Senggigi Square Blk B-10, T0370 693688, www.squarelombok.com. Open 1100-2400. Senggigi's concession to sophisticated dining, **Square** bills itself as a lounge restaurant, and has a decent wine list, good seafood and plenty of steaks to get your teeth into. They have a monthly cellar party – for US$30 you can drink as much wine and eat as many tapas dishes as you can handle.

$$ Ye Jeon Korean Restaurant, Senggigi Plaza, T0370 693059. Open 0930-2100. This Korean-owned eatery serves authentic Korean favourites such as *bibimbap* and *bulgogi*. The set meals are good value and filling.

$ Café Wayang, on the main road in Senggigi, T0370 693098. A branch of the one in Ubud, Bali, this building has character (complete with a family of mice in the rafters), but slow service.

$ Gelateria, Senggigi Plaza A1-04. Open 1000-1900. Perfect for a cheap lunch, offering lots of good Indonesian staples, including *bakso*, *nasi goreng*, and *mie goreng*. Also serves good coffee and home-made gelato to the strains of modern Indonesian rock music.

😊 Entertainment

Senggigi *p92*
If you really want to party, it would be better to wait until you get to the hedonist pleasures of Gili Trawangan, however, there are a couple of options in Senggigi. **Papaya Café**, Jln Raya Senggigi, T0370 693616. Open 1000-0100. Live music, serves pizza and steak and icy beer.

There are a few late-night options on Senggigi Square including **Gosip Discotique** (T0819 1734 1437, until 0400), which features 'super sexy dancers live', and the nearby **Club 69** (T0370 692211, 1300-0400), with private karaoke rooms and a disco.

🛍 Shopping

Senggigi *p92*
Senggigi Jaya, on the main road. Has everything from food to T-shirts, film and gifts at reasonable prices. There are a few boutique/craft shops that are less prone to haggling than the old-school vendors.

🔺 Activities and tours

Senggigi *p92*
Cycling
Lombok Biking Tour, Jln Raya Senggigi, T0370 692164, www.lombokbiking.com. Open 0830-1930. Seeing the countryside of Lombok on 2 wheels is highly recommended, and this outfit has a selection of half-day trips to Lengsar, Pusuk Pass, and southern Lombok, as well as a surprise ride of the day. Costs vary between US$13-35 depending on length.

Diving and snorkelling
Dream Divers, Jln Raya Senggigi, T0370 692047, www.dreamdivers.com. Dive trips to the Gilis and Nusa Penida and Tulamben in Bali, as well as trips to the waters of southern Lombok where hammerhead sharks can be seen. Each dive costs US$38. Also offers daily snorkelling trips to the Gilis with their dive boats for US$20.

Tour operators
Bidy Tour, Jln Raya Senggigi, T0370 693521. Full-day fishing trips. International and domestic flight ticketing.
Perama, Jln Raya Senggigi, T0370 693007.

Trekking
Perama, Jln Raya Senggigi, T0370 693007. All-inclusive treks to Rinjani's summit, leaving from Senggigi at 0500. Treks cost between US$250 and US$300 depending on the number of nights. Minimum of 2 people.
Rinjani Trekking Club, Jln Raya Senggigi, T0370 693202, www.anaklombok.com. Senggigi is a good place to plan your

ascent of Gunung Rinjani, and this place offers a variety of trips. Their 2-day trip to the summit costs US$200, the same as their 3-day trip. All costs include guide service, accommodation, transfers and food. Recommended.

⊖ Transport

Senggigi p92
Bemo
Bemos wait on Jln Salah Singkar in Ampenan to pick up fares for Senggigi Beach and north to **Mangsit**. Regular bemos link **Ampenan** with **Mataram**, **Cakranegara** and the main **Cakra** bemo terminal between 0600 and 1800, 5000Rp. From one end of Senggigi to the other costs 1500Rp. Perama has an office here (see Tour operators) and runs a bus service geared to travellers. Shuttles include **Kuta Lombok** for US$12.50, **Padangbai**, 1 daily, US$30, **Kuta** and **Nguarah Rai Airport**, 1 daily, US$35, and **Ubud**, 1 daily, US$35.

Boat
Dream Divers (see Activities and tours) are the Senggigi agent for **Gili Cat**, which has a fast ferry (1½ hrs) to **Padangbai** for US$69.

Car hire and motorbike hire
Cars cost US$15 per day; motorbikes US$5.

Taxi
Blue Bird Taxi (also known here as Lombok Taksi) T0370 627000.

Bangsal p93
Bemo
Regular connections from **Mataram** or the **Bertais** terminal in **Cakranegara**; take a bemo heading for Tanjung or Bayan. Bemos stop at the junction at Pemenang, take a dokar the last 1 km to the coast. From Pelabuhan Lombok there are no direct bemos; either charter one (US$15) or catch a bemo to the Bertais terminal in Cakranegara and then another travelling to Bayan/Tanjung. From the port of Lembar, it is easiest to club together and charter a bemo to Bangsal.

Bus
Perama Tour has regular connections with **Lembar**, as well as all-in bus/ferry tickets to most destinationss in **Bali** (**Kuta**, **Sanur**, **Ubud**, **Lovina** and **Candi Dasa**).

❶ Directory

Senggigi p92
Banks Senggigi Beach Hotel has a bank on site with exchange facilities for non-residents. Money changer at the Pacific Supermarket. ATMs can be found along Jln Raya Senggigi. **Internet** Millennium Internet, Jln Raya Senggigi; and Superstar Internet, Senggigi Plaza, Blk A2. Both 300Rp per min. **Medical services** Klinik Risa, Jln Pejanggik 115, Cakranegara, T0370 625560. 24 hrs emergency room, full hospital facilities. **Police** Tourist police: Jln Raya Senggigi, T0370 632733. **Post office** Jln Raya Senggigi, Mon-Thu 0730-1700, Fri-Sat 0730-1600.

Gili Islands

The three tropical island idylls that make up the Gili Islands lie off Lombok's northwest coast, 20-45 minutes by boat from Bangsal. They are now a well-established fixture on the southeast Asian trail. Known as the 'Gilis' or the 'Gili Islands' by many travellers, this only means 'the Islands' in Sasak. Most locals have accepted this Western corruption of their language and will understand where you want to go. Be extra careful swimming here as there are very strong currents between the islands.

Ins and outs → *Phone code: 0370.*

With the development of Bali into an international tourist resort, many backpackers have moved east and the Gilis are the most popular of the various alternatives. This is already straining the islands' limited sewerage and water infrastructures, and a walk into the interior of Gili Trawangan will reveal large amounts of rubbish strewn about. During the peak months between June and August, Gili Trawangan becomes particularly crowded and it is advisable to book accommodation in advance.

The attraction of the Gilis resides in their golden sand beaches and the best snorkelling and diving off Lombok – for the amateur the experience is breathtaking. However, the coral does not compare with locations such as Flores and Alor: large sections are dead or damaged (because of dynamite fishing and the effects of El Nino, which raised the temperature of the water). Gili Meno and Gili Air are very quiet, and there is little to do except sunbathe, snorkel, swim, or dive. Gili Trawangan has the same attractions, but has also developed a reputation for its raucous nightlife, the most vibrant in Lombok, and it is the most popular of the islands, particularly with backpackers.

There is no police presence on any of the islands. In the event of anything untoward happening, contact the island's *kepala desa* – the village head (guesthouses or any of the dive centres should be able to point you in the right direction).

Getting there

Regular boats from Bangsal (see page 93) to the Gilis wait until about 20 people have congregated for the trip to the islands. Boats can also be chartered for the journey, 45 minutes to Gili Trawangan, 30 minutes to Gili Meno, 20 minutes to Gili Air. In the morning there is rarely a long wait, but in the afternoon people have had to wait several hours. An alternative is to buy a combined bus-and-boat ticket with one of the shuttle bus companies.

Several dive centres around town have boats going directly from Teluk Nare to the Gilis. Enquire around town. This avoids the port of Bangsal. Enquire at the **Perama** office in Senggigi. There are various alternatives. It's also possible to charter a boat from Senggigi for around US$30. Within Lombok there are services from Mataram to the Gilis and from Senggigi to the Gilis. (From Senggigi, some of the dive centres operate boats throughout the day.) One of the more popular ways to get to the Gilis from Bali is the **Perama** ferry from Padangbai, which takes four hours and calls in at all three islands. This costs US$30 and departs at 1330. The cheapest way is to take the slow ferry to Lembar, a shuttle bus to Bangsal and then a public boat to the Gili of your choice. This takes seven to eight hours, and the ferry departs at 0900, and costs US$15 – enquire at tourist offices in Padangbai. **Gili Cat** (www.gilicat.com) has a fast service from Gili Trawangan to Padangbai (Jalan Silayukti, T0363 41441, 1½ hours, US$69) departing at 1130. **Bluewater Express** (www.bwsbali.com) runs fast ferries from Serangan Harbour in southern Bali. **Scoot Cruises** (www.scootcruise.com) runs a similar service from Sanur via Nusa Lembongan. Check their websites for latest schedule and prices.

Getting around

The islands are small enough to walk around. Even Gili Trawangan, the largest of the three, is little more than 2 km from end to end. Gili Air and Gili Trawangan are great for cycling with good tracks. Cidomo are the main form of transport used by locals for carrying goods; some

Gili Islands

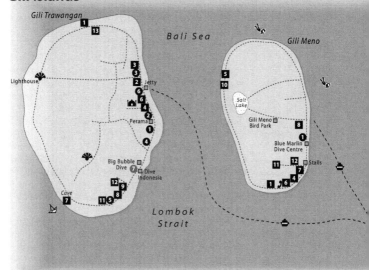

N

500 metres

500 yards

Gili Trawangan
Sleeping 🛏
Alam Gili **1**
Beach House **8**
Blue Beach Cottage **2**
Coral Beach 2 **13**

Dream Village **3**
Good Heart **3**
Kelapa Kecil **2**
Pondok Maulana **12**
Sama Sama
  Bungalows **6**
Snapper Bungalows **4**
Sunset Cottages **7**
Tir Na Nog **9**
Trawangan Cottages **12**
Villa Ombak **11**
Warna Homestay **2**

Eating 🍴
Blue Marlin &
  Dive School **1**
Coco **2**
Horizontal **3**
Pesona **4**
Scallywags **5**
Wrap A Snapper **6**

Bars & clubs 🍸
Rudy's **7**

Gili Meno
Sleeping 🛏
Biru Meno **1**
Gazebo **4**
Goodheart **5**
Kontiki **6**
Mallia's Child **7**
Mimpi Manis **8**
Sunset Gecko **10**
Tao Kombo **11**
Villa Nautilus **12**

offer round-island trips costing around 50,000Rp, although costs are very negotiable. There is a shuttle service between the islands, with tickets that can be bought at the ticket office at the harbour of each island Boats leave Gili Meno for Gili Trawangan at 0815 and 1520, from Gili Meno to Gili Air at 0950 and 1620. From Gili Air to Gili Meno at 0830 and 1500 and from Gili Air to Gili Trawangan at 0830 and 1500. There are departures from Gili Trawangan to Gili Meno at 0930 and 1600 and to Gili Air at 0930 and 1600. Fares for shorter hops (neighbouring islands) start at 18,000Rp, from Gili Air to Gili Trawangan, the most expensive trip, the fare is 25,000Rp.

Gili Trawangan → For listings, see pages 101-107.

The largest of the three islands – and the furthest west from Bangsal – is Gili Trawangan (Dragon Island). It is the most interesting island because of its hill in the centre; there are several trails to the summit and excellent views over to Mount Rinjani on Lombok from the top. In the opposite direction, you can watch the sun set over Mount Agung on Bali.

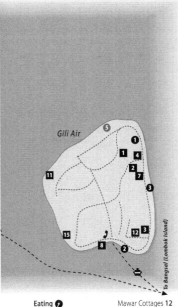

There is a coastal path around the island, which takes about 2½ hours to walk. Originally a penal colony, it now supports the greatest number of tourist bungalows. These are mostly concentrated along its east coast, as are a number of restaurants (serving good seafood) and bars. For lone travellers seeking company, this is the best island. But Gili Trawangan is in danger of ruining itself (like so many other tropical island idylls in the region). Indeed, for some it already has. The most developed area is brash, loud and over-developed, but the island is large enough to offer peace and tranquillity as well. Gili Air and Gili Meno are quieter.

The most luxurious accommodation is found in the developed southeast area of the island behind the restaurants; locals already refer to it being like Kuta, although this is an exaggeration. Here you can find well-equipped air-conditioned bungalows with cable TV and personal chefs; unfortunately you lose the peace and beauty associated with a small, relatively undeveloped island, as the accommodation is hidden behind the noisy restaurants away from the beach. To find a quiet tropical paradise, visitors have to accept more basic facilities at the outer edges of the developed areas, particularly the north and northeastern strip of coast, which remains accessible. Here guests can hear the waves

Eating 🍴
Rust Warung **1**

Gili Air
Sleeping 🛏
Abdi Fantastik **4**
Coconut Cottages &
 Frangipani Restaurant **2**
Gili Air Santay &
 Restaurant **7**
Gili Indah **8**
Lucky's **15**
Matahari **11**

Mawar Cottages **12**
Sejuk Cottages **1**
Sunrise Cottages **3**

Eating 🍴
Blue Marlin
 & Dive Centre **1**
Go Go Cafe **2**
Green Café **3**

Bars & clubs 🍸
Space Bar **5**

lapping against the shore and the birds singing, watch stuning sunrises and sunsets from their verandas and believe they are in paradise. Room rates triple at some of the more upmarket places in the high season. Even off-peak rooms can become scarce, so it is worth arriving on the island early. The cheapest accommodation can be found away from the beach, along the lanes in the village. Gili Trawangan offers the best choice of restaurants of the three Gilis, and many people consider that it has the best snorkelling. Snorkelling is good off the east shore, particularly at the point where the shelf drops away near **Horizontal** and at the north end of the beach.

Inland from the tourist strip is the original village where life goes on almost as usual, a world apart from the tourists and therefore interesting to stroll through. Further inland there are scattered farms among the coconut groves that dominate the interior, and some pleasant walks to be had.

Safety Given the conservative nature of Lombok, women should abstain from topless sunbathing. There have been plenty of reports of women being hassled by local men, and it is not wise to set off on long walks alone in the dark. Also, single women should keep an eye on their drinks in bars, to make sure nothing is slipped in. It is unlikely that this would happen, but not unheard of.

Gili Meno → For listings, see pages 101-107.

Gili Meno (Snake Island), between Trawangan and Air, is the smallest of the islands, and also the quietest and least developed. The local residents are very friendly, and after half a day on the island most will know your name and where you stay. The disadvantage of staying on Gili Meno is that the hawker to tourist ratio is very high, so expect plenty of visits from trinket sellers (often the same ones repeatedly).

The snorkelling off Gili Meno – especially off the northeast coast – is considered by some to be better than Trawangan, with growths of rare blue coral. There is a path running round the island; a walk of one to 1½ hours. The salt lake in the northeast of the island provides a breeding ground for mosquitoes. Accommodation on Gili Meno tends to be more expensive than on the other two islands. Some of the guesthouse owners live on Lombok, and these bungalows are run by lads who are poorly paid and consequently have little motivation. However, the views from the many bungalows that face the sea are beautiful, especially towards the east and Mount Rinjani.

Gili Meno Bird Park
ⓘ *T0361 287727, www.balipvbgroup.com, 0800-1700, 50,000Rp adult, 25,000Rp child, follow the signposted path near the harbour through the middle of the island, it's a 10-min walk.*
The 2500-sq-m aviary contains over 300 species of birds, and offers interactive feeding times and guided tours. There are also komodo dragons, kangaroos and plenty of turtles. This makes for a nice break from the monotony of beaches for kids, and the **Cavern Bar**, filled with Beatles memorabilia, is a good spot for mums and dads to take a break.

Gili Air → For listings, see pages 101-107.

Gili Air (Turtle Island) is the easternmost island, lying closest to Bangsal. It has the largest local population, with a village of around 400 families in the centre of the island. The island takes about an hour to walk around. As the local population is Muslim, visitors should

Seaweed farming

Seaweed farming is being encouraged off Gili Air as an alternative to fishing, in order to protect the coral. Although laws against the use of dynamite fishing were passed in 1984, some fishermen still use it as well as stones to kill the fish, damaging the coral in the process. The waters round the island provide suitable conditions for seaweed farming: there is a good flow of water, but the reef protects the area from strong currents; the considerable depth of the Lombok Strait keeps sea temperatures from becoming too high and keeps salinity at a constant level. These are all prerequisites for the successful cultivation of seaweed. From the fishermens' viewpoint, seaweed farming has the attraction of being less hard work than fishing. The green Kotoni variety is grown and is exported for use.

The seaweed is farmed by fixing posts in the shallow seabed. Rope is attached to these posts, making a frame about 2 m sq. At roughly 30 cm intervals nodules of seaweed containing a seedhead are tied onto the rope using strips of shredded plastic bags. The seaweed must remain covered by water, so the ropes are held afloat just under the surface using plastic bottles, which are due to be replaced by more visually pleasing lengths of bamboo. After 40 days the seaweed is harvested and dried; 7 kg of wet seaweed producing 1 kg dry weight. This is then sold on Lombok for 800Rp per kg (or an equivalent value in rice and coffee), each family producing about 50 kg. Cuttings from the harvested seaweed are retained to grow into the next crop.

avoid topless sunbathing. Despite the number of bungalows, it remains a peaceful place to stay. Snorkelling is quite good off the island. When leaving your accommodation take sensible precautions and make sure you lock both the door to the bathroom and the front door. As most bathrooms have no roofs, a favoured way for thieves to gain entry is over the bathroom wall and into your room via the bathroom door.

Gili Islands listings

For Sleeping and Eating price codes and other relevant information, see pages 7-10.

● Sleeping

In the past few years, many foreigners have invested in the Gilis, resulting in a wide range of accommodation options. Many bungalows are being upgraded. Of the more basic ones there is often little difference – they tend to charge the same rates, and the huts are similar in design and size, attractively built out of local materials, in a local style, mostly raised on stilts. Mosquitoes can be a problem at certain times of year and mosquito nets

are routinely provided. The most luxurious bungalows fall into our **$$$$** category. Friendliness and the cleanliness of the *mandis* tends to be the deciding factor at the basic bungalows. The higher the price, the more likely tax and service charge will be extra, and the less likely breakfast will be included. During the peak months Jun-Aug it can be difficult to get a room, so arrive early in the day. Tips on where to stay from travellers are probably your best bet. The coastal strip on the easten side of each island is the most developed. Peace, solitude and outrageous sunsets can be found on the western side of each island. Unless otherwise stated, all bungalows have private bathrooms with shower. Fresh-water resources are scarce on the islands so water in the bathrooms can often be saline, as it is taken from wells. However, some places offer fresh-water showers. All prices quoted here are low season. Expect them to double during the high season.

Gili Trawangan *p99, map p98*

$$$$ Kelapa Kecil, T0812 375 6003, www.kelapavillas.com. Sleek and stylish but lacking island grace, the 3 a/c rooms here are popular, and have great sea views. Small pool.

$$$$ Villa Ombak, T0370 642336, www.hotelombak.com. Selection of 60 rooms, some in beautiful *lumbung*-style cottages set in well-tended gardens. The water here is saline, although they provide a jar of fresh water for guests to use to rinse off any residue after showering. These a/c rooms have large open bathroom, TV, and the more expensive *lumbung* cottages have a downstairs living area, and balcony with loungers. Full spa service, restaurant, pool and diving centre.

$$$$-$$$ Tir Na Nog, T0370 639463, www.tirnanogbar.com. 10 comfortable and spacious a/c rooms with hot water set behind the popular bar. There is also a 2 bedroom villa available with small pool.

$$$$-$$ The Beach House, T0370 642352, www.beachhousegilit.com. This Australian-owned hotel is going from strength to strength, with its 12 bungalows and 3 villas currently being added to. The cheaper a/c rooms are comfortable, and have private terrace and cable TV. However, it's the villas here that are a steal, offering privacy and featuring fresh-water plunge pool, kitchenette, cable TV and space for 4 in tastefully decorated rooms. Consistently booked out well in advance, so reservations are essential. Fresh-water swimming pool. Recommended.

$$$ Alam Gili, T0370 630 466, www.alam indahbali.com. Set on the quiet northern shore, and near some good snorkelling, the Alam Gili is a well-managed establishment with cool, breezy Balinese-style bungalows with sea views and access to a salt-water jungle pool. This is a good retreat from the more hedonistic central strip. Those in need of some action can get into 'town' in around 20 mins on a cidomo.

$$$ Dream Village, T0370 664 4373. www.dreamvillagetrawangan.it. The 5 large a/c bungalows have cable TV and fine sunrise views, but are a little overpriced. There are are 6 Balinese-style rooms. Reservations necessary.

$$$ Sama Sama Bungalows, T0812 376 3650, www.thesamasama.com. 4 a/c *lumbung* bungalows with high ceilings and tasteful decor. There is a bar in front playing live acoustic music, which the friendly owner insists stops at 0100.

$$ Blue Beach Cottage, T0370 263846. Located next to Trawangan's finest stretch of beach, the stylish a/c bungalows have huge bathrooms, high ceilings and mosquito nets. The staff are very friendly.

$$ Good Heart, T0370 663 0239, goodheart-trawangan@hotmail.com. No relation to the bungalows on Gili Meno, the comfortable a/c *lumbung* cottages are a stone's throw from the beach, with cool outdoor bathroom and good views from the private balcony. Rooms have cable TV, fridge and safety box.

$$ Snapper Bungalows, T0370 624417, www.beachhousegilit.com/snapper_bungalows.html. Located just behind Wrap a Snapper fish n' chip shop, the Snapper has a decent selection of fan and a/c rooms with outdoor terrace. Guests can also use the swimming pool and facilities at the Beach House Resort.

$ Coral Beach 2, T0370 639946. Well located at the quiet northern end of the island, and near good snorkelling, the rooms here are simple and quite clean. There is a restaurant attached serving good pizza and icy drinks.

$ Melati Bungalows, T0852 3952 1697. This laid-back place has 4 simple fan rooms with friendly staff.

$ Pondok Maulana, T0817 574 6118, www.
pondokmaulana.bravehost.com. 4 spotless
rooms, with large veranda. Popular.

$ Sunset Cottages T0812 378 5290. Simple
bungalows with 2 beds, mosquito nets,
hammocks on balconies. Situated on the
western side of the island, taking advantage
of the splendid sunsets featuring Mount
Agung on Bali as a breathtaking backdrop.
Very peaceful. It's about a 40-min walk into
'town' for other restaurants and shopping,
or take a cidomo (if you can find one).

$Trawangan Cottages, T0370 623582.
Also in the village, lodgings here are
popular and convenient for the bars
along the main strip. Rooms are clean.

$ Warna Homestay, T0370 623859. 7 clean
and comfortable rooms with plenty of light.

Gili Meno *p100, map p98*

$$$ Villa Nautilus, T0370 642143, www.
villanautilus.com. Beautifully designed
private cottages facing the sea, with
outside terrace, some with sea views. The
room has a living area, and the large bed
is on a raised platform, with good quality
fabrics used for bedding and curtains.

$$$-$$ Gazebo, T0370 635795. Set in
forest, with its own stretch of beach with
loungers, the well spaced out cottages
look dreary from the outside, yet internally
are spacious, well furnished and tastefully
decorated with Indonesian artefacts.
There is a small pool next the to the beach.

$$$-$$ Kontiki, T0370 632824. Used by
tourists on **Perama** tours, near the beach,
with large and clean rooms. The staff are
a great source of local information and
very friendly. Some rooms have fresh
water shower and space to sleep 3 people.

$$$-$ The Sunset Gecko, T0815 766418,
www.thesunsetgecko.com. This Japanese-
owned place blows all the Meno
competition out of the water with
its innovative eco-friendly ideals,
unconventional communal washbasins,
outdoor showers and toilets (very clean and
secure) and comfortable accommodation

in thatched bungalows. There is a
2-storey house with amazing views of Gili
Trawangan and Gunung Agung from its
terrace at sunset, that is often booked for
weeks at a time. If you want the house, it is
necessary to reserve well in advance. Good
snorkelling offshore. Recommended.

$$ Biru Meno, T08133 975 8968, www.biru
meno.com. At the southern end of the main
beach strip, the 8 bungalows here are set
in a very tranquil location and seem rather
underused. Fan rooms have sea view.

$$ Goodheart, T0813 3655 6976. Located
on the western side of the island, the 5
2-storey *lumbung* cottages have precipitous
stairs leading up to a simple bedroom.
Access to the bathroom is through a
trapdoor in the bedroom floor. A great
beachside *berguga* (seating pavilion) to
watch the sunset.

$$ Mallia's Child, T0370 622007, www.gili
meno-mallias.com. These bungalows are
right on the beach with excellent views
over to Gili Air and Lombok. Rooms are
clean, though a little small. Tax not included
in the price. Slightly overpriced. Rates fall
with a little gentle negotiation.

$$ Mimpi Manis, T0817 997 9579. Very
spacious thatched bungalows with large
balcony and hammock set in a large garden.
Rooms come with a Bahasa Indonesia
coursebook so guests can mingle with the
locals better. Fresh-water shower. Breakfast
and tax are not included in the price.

$$ Tao Kombo, T0812 372 2174, www.tao-
kombo.com/uk/presentation.htm. Away
from the beach in a forest clearing, there
is plenty of birdsong here. The *lumbung*
bungalows are filled with light, and have
high ceilings. The location is very peaceful,
and the hotel offers lots of boardgames
and a book exchange. Recommended.

Gili Air *p100, map p98*

To make the most of this 'paradise' island it's
best to stay in one of the bungalows dotted
around the coast within sound and sight of
the sea. There's also accommodation inland

from the point where the boats land on the south coast, but this does not offer sea views.

$$$-$$ Coconut Cottages, T0370 635365, www.coconuts-giliair.com. Owned by a friendly Glasgow native and her husband, the 7 a/c and fan rooms here are great value, with well-designed interiors and huge bathrooms. The beds are king size, and there are reading lights. Recommended.

$$ Hotel Gili Indah, T0370 637328. Comfortable fan and a/c rooms with sea views close to the harbour and handy for quiet walks on the island's west.

$$ Lucky's, on the west side of the island, T0819 3316 0613, about a 15-min walk to the harbour. This friendly place doesn't get as much business as it ought to, given the marvellous sunset views and quiet vibes on offer. Fan and a/c rooms.

$$ Sejuk Cottages, T0370 636461, www.sejukcottages.com. Down a path off the eastern side of the island, this hotel has a good selection of clean bungalows with spacious verandas. The more expensive feature TV and a/c.

$$ Sunrise Cottages, T0370 642370. Set in a garden so parched that walking through it makes you feel thirsty. This hotel has a good, wide selection of rooms and the choice ones are often full. The 2-storey *lumbung* have an outdoor lounge area downstairs and an outdoor bathroom.

$$-$ Gili Air Santay, T0818 0375 8695, www.giliair-santay.com. Has a loyal following of regular Gili Air visitors, lured by the efficient Austrian management and simple yet comfortable bungalows. There are no locks on some of the bathroom doors.

$ Abdi Fantastik, T0370 622179. Simple bungalows with room for 3 people. All have sea view. Friendly staff. Good swimming and snorkelling offshore.

$ Matahari, 25-min walk from the harbour along the western coastal path. For serious seekers of isolation only, this simple place on the west coast is a great spot to leave the world behind, chat with local fishermen and watch clouds drift by. The owners can prepare decent Indonesian meals.

$ Mawar Cottages, T0813 6225 3995. These guys will probably meet you off the boat and try to entice you to stay at their lodgings, which are set away from the beach in a quiet garden. This is definite backpacker territory and an acoustic guitar looms ominously on the wall of the large communal area. All rooms with mosquito net and fan, although cheaper rooms feature squat toilet.

🍴 Eating

The choice of food is best on Gili Trawangan. A number of restaurants serving excellent seafood, particularly fish; the specials board will tell you the day's fresh catch. There are basic provision shops on all the islands selling snacks and some fresh fruit.

Gili Trawangan *p99, map p98*

$$ The Beach House, T0370 642352, www.beachhousegilit.com. Open 24 hrs. Popular beachfront eatery serving fish kebabs, pies and quiches, tasty home-made soups and some Indonesian dishes. Fresh seafood is laid out around 1800 and diners pick their choice.

$$ Blue Marlin, T0370 632424. Open 0800-2300. Extremely popular place with good portions of Western food, fresh seafood and a decent vegetarian menu.

$$ Horizontal, T0878 63039727. Open 0800-2300. An attempt at Seminyak style, which looks a little faded during daytime, but comes into its own as the sunsets. Good range of fare including pan-fried fillet of white snapper, Japanese tuna rolls, Thai curries and banoffee pie.

$$ Pesona, T0370 6607233, www.pesonaresort.com. Open 0800-2300. The owners are of Indian origin and you will find the best veg and non-veg Indian grub in the Gilis here. The *masala dosa* adds a few southern Indian vibes to the proceedings. It doubles up as a sheesha bar at night, where you can puff away on apple tobacco.

\$\$ Scallywags, T0370 631945. Open 0800-2300. Beautifully designed restaurant, with some seating on the beach. The menu features delights such warm goat's cheese salad, Basque tapas dishes and plenty of fresh seafood. Good wine selection. Recommended.

\$\$ Tir Na Nog, T0370 639463, www.tirna nogbar.com. Open 0800-2300. Popular for pizza, steak-and-Guiness pie and with a decent vegetarian selection.

\$\$ Wrap A Snapper, T0370 624217. Open 0800-2200. Australian-owned, serving up fish 'n' chips, battered snacks and fish burgers, plus some healthy options! Will deliver food to diners to the beach for 5000Rp.

\$ Coco, T0813 5353 5737. Open 0700-1800. Ideal spot for a light lunch, this small and efficient café prepares baguettes with tasty fillings such as roasted vegetables and feta cheese. The small salad menu is dreamy, with offerings like spicy smoked marlin salad. Good coffee selection. Recommended.

Gili Meno *p100, map p98*

The gourmet scene in Gili Meno is very quiet with eating mainly restricted to hotel restaurants, which can be highly variable in quality. Places close when the last patron leaves, which can be early.

\$\$ Villa Nautilus, T0370 642124. Open 0700-2100. Good salads and pasta on offer with friendly service. Does a rather doughy wood-fired pizza smothered in cheese, if that's your thing.

\$\$-\$ Good Heart, T0813 3655 6976. Open 0700-2100. Fresh seafood including barracuda, tuna, snapper and some vegetarian dishes such as tofu curry. There is a good cocktail list.

\$\$-\$ Rust Warung, T0370 642324. Open 0700-2100. Cheap sandwiches, soups and local favourites, but really comes alive at night when the local boys lay out the fresh fish for patrons to choose. There's a good atmosphere and many diners linger after eating to enjoy the cool breeze and a Bintang.

\$ Mallia's Child, T0370 622007. Open 0700-2100. Cheap Indonesian fare, reasonable Thai curries and home-made soup.

\$ Sunset Gecko, T0815 766418. Open 0700-2100. Local Sasak cuisine, some Western food and a delicious vegetarian red curry.

Gili Air *p100, map p98*

Many restaurants cater primarily to Western tastes and the 'Indonesian' food is often disappointingly bland.

\$\$ Blue Marlin, T0370 634387. Hungry divers head here for good-quality Western food served in large portions.

\$\$ Frangipani (see Sleeping), T0370 635365. Open 0800-2200. Lots of tasty Indonesian, international and some Sasak cuisine served in a friendly, clean setting. Recommended.

\$\$-\$ Gili Air Santay, T0818 0375 8695. Open 0700-2200. Excellent array of Thai dishes and other Asian favourites served from a spotless kitchen. This laid-back place is deservedly popular and social. Recommended.

\$ Go Go Café, T0817 570 8337. Open 0700-2400. Not far from the harbour, this breezy eatery dishes up fair Indonesian staples, pizza and pasta dishes. Slow service.

\$ Green Café, T0818 365954. Open 0800-2300. This beachside joint is a good place to sample some Sasak cuisine, such as *urap urap* (vegetables in a coconut sauce). Also prepares fresh seafood dishes and has a lovely home-made yoghurt. Movies are often shown in the evenings.

♪ Bars and clubs

Gili Trawangan *p99, map p98*

There is plenty of nocturnal action available, with local boys competing with foreigners for the attention of female visitors. Many places have a designated party night that goes on until the wee hours. Be careful of the magic mushroom milkshakes on sale in many places, they can be very strong and Lombok is a long way from home.

Horizontal, T0878 6303 9727. Open 0700-0200. Cool lounge setting, plenty of drinks deals and chilled house music by the beach.
Rudy's Bar, T0370 642311. Open 0800-0200. Popular with the backpacking set, this is the place to get feral, with plenty of reggae and house, happy hour 1500-2200.
Sama Sama, T0812 376 3650. Open 1900-0100. This friendly bar has chilled acoustic music in a mellow setting close to the beach.
Tir Na Nog, T0370 639463. Open 0700-0200 except Wed 0700-sunrise. This Irish theme bar is cavernous, and caters for every whim, to the point where it almost becomes overwhelming. There is a darts board, table football, scattering of *beruga* with small TV and DVD player with an extensive film library, huge TV showing live football and a DJ spinning tunes nightly from 2100. Has a weekly party on Wed nights.

Gili Air *p100, map p98*

Most people are here to relax rather than get wild, so the beachfront restaurants double up as bars in the evening, and can be a great way to meet people. **Gili Air Santay** (see Eating) is recommended.
Space Bar, T0812 378 7254. Open 0700-2300 except Wed 0700-sunrise. Harking back to mid-1990s Goa trance days, the walls of this small bar are festooned with fluorescent paintings of dolphins leaping from the sea and naughty-looking mushrooms. The Wed night party comes with a complete DJ line up until sunrise. Happy hour is 1700-1900.

⊕ Entertainment

Gili Trawangan *p99, map p98*
Beautiful Life, open 1000-2400. On the busy southeastern coastal strip, this place offers movies in a darkened outdoor cinema, and personal movie booths on the beach side of the road where you can select a film from their library. You must buy some food or a drink to watch a film.

▲▲ Activities and tours

Gili Islands *p97, map p98*
Body and soul
Massage is available at many guesthouses and hotels on all 3 islands. Gili Trawangan has a few spa and massage places including **Villa Ombak**, T0370 642336, which has the most comprehensive spa and massage service.

Cycling
Gili Air and Gili Trawangan make superb places to get lost along island tracks, or follow the coastal paths for stunning views and peace and quiet. Bikes can be rented on Gili Air for 30,000Rp a day, and on Gili Trawangan for 35,000Rp a day.

Diving and snorkelling
While the diving here may not be quite as good as that in some other parts of Indonesia, it is ideal for less experienced divers as many of the dives are no deeper than 18 m and the waters are calm. Best diving conditions are late Apr-Aug. Good diving spots include **Shark Point** with white-and-black tipped reef sharks, sea snakes and turtles; **Meno Wall**, famed for turtles and nudibranches; and Air Slope, with its population of ghost pipe fish, frog fish and leaf scorpion fish. The dive centres on all 3 islands have formed an association to monitor control of diving on the islands, and protection of the reefs. Prices are the same at all schools, so as to maintain high standards and safety. Example costs are US$35 for a guided fun dive (must be certified diver), PADI Open Water US$350, Advanced Open Water US$275, Discover Scuba US$60, and Dive Master US$650, with unlimited dives over a 1-month period. **Big Bubble Dive**, T0370 625020, www.big bubblediving.com. Has courses in numerous European languages, and is highly regarded. **Blue Marlin**, T0812 376 6496, www.blue marlindive.com. Has dive schools on all 3

islands, and offers a free pool try-out for anyone interested in diving at their centres in Gili Trawangan and Gili Air. On Trawangan.

Snorkels and fins can be hired for 25,000Rp from many of the *losmen* or vendors along the beach. The snorkelling off Gili Trawangan is marginally the best; be careful off Gili Meno, as the tide is strong and the water is shallow, and it is easy to get swept onto the coral. Many agencies on all 3 islands offer snorkelling trips around all 3 islands in a glass-bottomed boat for 80,000-100,000Rp. This trip is highly recommended.

Fishing
Night fishing can be organized from several places on Gili Air. Try **Abdi Fantastik** (see Sleeping), which has speargun fishing trips from 1800-2200, costing US40 per person.

Kayaking
Kayaking Alberto, the owner of Dream Village, T0370 664 4373, rents out sea kayaks for 45,000Rp per day.

Tour operators
Perama, T0370 638514, has their own office near the harbour on Gili Trawangan. On Gili Meno they can be found at the **Kontiki Hotel**, T0370 632824, and on Gili Air at the **Hotel Gili Indah**, T0370 637328.

⊖ Transport

Gili Islands *p97, map p98*
Don't purchase bus tickets to Senggigi or other Lombok destinations on the islands, they are more expensive. You can purchase a ticket on a shuttle bus to Senggigi or Mataram at Bangsal for 40,000Rp. The shuttle bus touts will find you when you get off the boat. Be firm in your bargaining.

Boat
Public boats from the islands to **Bangsal** leave when full, except for Giili Meno, which has 2 sailings a day to Bangsal at 0800 and 1400 approximately; buy your ticket at the harbour. For onward connections to **Bali**, arrive at the ticket booth by 0730. At Bangsal you can also book through to Bali with one of the shuttle bus companies. The 'Island Hopping' boat makes 2 round trips a day connecting the islands.

To **Bali**, **Perama** has bus-boat ticket combination tickets. The direct **Perama** boat to **Padangbai** departs at 0700 and costs US$30. Also has connections to other destinations in Bali. **Gili Cat**, www.gilicat. com, sails direct from Gili Trawangan to **Padangbai** in 1½ hrs for 1100, US$69. **Bluewater Express** (www.bwsbali.com) sails directly to Serangan Harbour in southern Bali (US$69) and **Scoot Cruises** sail directly to Sanur (US$65). Check websites for schedules.

❶ Directory

Gili Islands *p97, map p98*
Banks It is best to change money before leaving the mainland as rates are more expensive on the islands. There are money changers on all 3 islands. **Internet** On Gili Meno, there is a small place in the centre of the island opposite the Bird Park charging 500Rp per min. On Gili Trawangan there are numerous places with high-speed internet. Tara, 0800-2300, is near the harbour. On Gili Air there is internet access at the wartel next to Coconut Cottages. **Medical services** There is a small clinic on Gili Meno near the Bird Park. On Gili Trawangan there is a good clinic at Villa Ombak, T0370 642336. The doctor visits from the mainland on Tue, Thu and Sat. **Post office** There is a post box at the Gili Indah Hotel on Gili Air, where the boat docks. William's Bookshop on Gili Trawangan is also a postal agent. Each island has a wartel. On Gili Air you can make phone calls at the wartel next to Coconut Cottages.

Northwest coast and Mount Rinjani

Following the coast north from Pemenang and Bangsal, the road passes the turn-off for Sir each (about 2 km north of Pemenang). This northwest coast is little touched by tourism and there are several 'traditional' villages where the more adventurous tour companies take visitors. The best-known of these is Bayan, at the foot of Mount Rinjani's northern slopes and about 50 km from Pemenang. Mount Rinjani, rising to 3726 m, dominates north Lombok.

Northwest coast → *For listings, see page 110.*

Siri Beach

Siri beach is down a dirt track – to the left are coconut plantations – and reaches the deserted, long, narrow strip of soft, white sand on a headland looking across to Gili Air. Take all food and drink: there are no facilities here. This is worth a visit to get away from the crowds. To get there, take a bemo running north from Pemanang; the walk to the beach is about 2 km from the road.

Bayan

This is a traditional Sasak village and the birthplace of Lombok's unique Muslim 'schism' – *Islam Waktu Telu*. There is a mosque here that is believed to be 300 years old. The village is the jumping-off point for climbs up Mount Rinjani (see below). There is no accommodation.

Mount Rinjani → *For listings, see page 110.*

Visitors who have made the effort invariably say that the highlight of their stay on Lombok was climbing Mount Rinjani. The views from the summit on a clear day are simply breathtaking. The ascent requires three days (although some keen climbers try to do it in two). Be warned that the summit is often wreathed in cloud, and views down to the blue-green lake within the caldera are also often obscured by a layer of cloud that lies trapped in the enormous crater.

Mount Rinjani is the second-highest mountain in Indonesia outside Irian Jaya – rising to an altitude of 3726 m. The volcano is still active but last erupted some time ago – in 1901, although in 1997 rumblings left dust raining for a week. The mountain, and a considerable area of land surrounding the mountain totalling some 400 sq km, has been gazetted as a national park.

The climb

There are two routes up Mount Rinjani. The easier and more convenient begins about 2 km to the west of the village of Bayan, on the way to Anyer. The track leads upwards from the road to the small settlement of **Batu Koq** and from there, 1 km on, to another village, **Senaru**. Tents, equipment and guides or porters can be hired in either of these two settlements (ask at the *losmen*); accommodation is available. It is recommended that trekkers check in at the conservation office in Senaru before beginning the ascent. A guide is not essential as the trail is well marked from Senaru to the crater rim; however, suitable climbing gear is required. From Senaru, the trek to the summit takes about two days, or 10 hours solid climbing. On the trek up, the path passes through stands of teak and mahogany, then into pine forest and lichin. There are stunning views from the lip of the crater down to the beautiful blue-green and mineral rich lake, **Segara Anak** (Child of the Sea), below. A third day is needed to walk down into the caldera. The caldera is 8 km long by 5 km wide.

On the east side of the lake is **Mount Baru** (New Mountain), an active cone within a cone that rose out of the lake in 1942. It can be reached by boat and the climb to Mount Baru's summit, through a wasteland of volcanic debris, is rewarded with a view into this secondary crater. Along the base of the main crater are numerous hot springs including **Goa Susu** (Milk Cave – so called because of its colour), which are reputed to have spectacular healing powers. Bathing in them is a good way to round off a tiring descent.

An alternative and more difficult route up the mountain – but some climbers claim it is more interesting – is via **Sembalun Lawang**, **Sembalun Bumbung** or **Sapit** on the mountain's eastern slopes. This alternative route is less well marked. A guide is recommended to show climbers the route to the second rim. There is accommodation here and guides are also available, but there is a shortage of equipment for hire. There is food available to buy for the trek but the range is not as good as in Senaru. To get to Sembalun Bumbung, take a bus from Labuhan Lombok. The climb to the crater takes about nine hours. For ambitious climbers who intend to reach the true summit of Mount Rinjani – rather than just the caldera – this is the better of the two routes. **Note** In the past, some embassies in Jakarta have advised visitors not to climb Mount Rinjani because of fears of violent theft. However, no one going up, nor the guides, seemed concerned or particularly aware of any great problems. Nonetheless, check before beginning the climb.

It's also possible to do a **round trip**, taking in both sides of the mountain. Each side of Rinjani offers its own character and a recommended alternative is to climb up the eastern flank and down the western. To do this, go to Senaru to rent equipment and buy supplies (the choice is best here), return to Anyer or Bayan and take a bemo or ojek to Sembalun Lawang. (Start early, bemos to Sembalun Lawang are rare after 1600.) Hire a guide and porter in Sembalun Lawang and stay the night. The next day the guide can show the route to the second rim (six to seven hours); from here, the climb to the summit (three to four hours) and then down into the caldera (three hours), and from there up to the first rim and back down to Senaru (six to seven hours), is well marked and the guide is not needed.

Best time to climb The best time is from May to November, during the dry season, when it is less likely to be cloudy. Do not attempt the climb during the rainy season as the trail can be treacherous. The climb, though not technically difficult, is arduous and climbers should be in reasonable physical condition. **Recommended equipment**: water, sweater and coat, foam camping roll, sleeping bag, tough walking shoes, food/supplies, firewood (there is increasing evidence of climbers chopping down trees within this national park in order to light a fire). *Please* take all your litter with you. **Note** Some climbers have complained of the poor quality of equipment hired in Senaru; check it carefully. A tent and/or sleeping bag hired for the guide would be greatly appreciated; it's cold on the mountain.

There is a US$16.50 admission fee to the Gunung Rinjani National Park, that needs to be paid at either the **Rinjani Trekking Club**① *T0868 1210 4132, www.rinjanitrekkingclub. com*, in Senaru, or at the **Rinjani Information Centre** in Sembalun Lawang. This is normally included in the price of a trek package, but make sure before you sign off. You can also rent any necessary equipment at these places. Treks can be arranged in Senaru through the **Rinjani Trekking Club**, or through one of the local guides. A reasonable package including guide fee and entrance fee would be around US$150-200 for a two-day/one-night ascent and up to US$300 for a longer four-day/three-night trek. Package rates fall in the low season. Treks can also be arranged in Senggigi with the reputable **Rinjani Trekking Club** (see Activities and tours, page 95). Their prices are very reasonable and are all-inclusive. Alternatively, you can book treks up Gunung Rinjani at any of the Perama offices. They have a variety of treks that depart from **Senggigi**, see page 95.

Northwest coast and Mount Rinjani listings

For Sleeping and Eating price codes and other relevant information, see pages 7-10.

🛏 Sleeping

Mount Rinjani *p108*
It is possible to stay at Batu Koq and Senaru, as well as at Sembalun Lawang if making the climb from the east. Senaru has the best selection of *losmen* (basic, all **$$-$**) and new ones seem to open almost every month.
Bale Bayan Guesthouse, T0817 579 2943. Near the mountain, clean and friendly, the owner speaks reasonable English and German. Recommended.
Batu Koq Pondok, Segara Anak, T0817 575 4551. Has been recommended. Price includes breakfast and supper; some exquisite views.
Pondok Senaru, T0868 1210 4141. Clean, well run, big restaurant, ice-cold *mandi*.
Pondok Gunung Baru, T0819 3312 8229. 5 clean rooms. Good trekking information.
Rinjani Trekking Club, contact their Senggigi office, T0370 693860, and **Emy Homestay**. Both have simple lodging.

🎉 Festivals and events

Mount Rinjani *p108*
Dec In the 2nd week of Dec, the **Pakelem**, offering feast is held on Segara Anak to ask for God's blessings.

⛰ Activities and tours

Mount Rinjani *p108*
Tours
The most convenient way to climb Rinjani is by booking a place on a tour. Several tour operators in Senggigi (see page 95) and on the Gilis organize climbs (US$150-250 all in). Tours are also available from *losmen* at various villages.

🚌 Transport

Bayan *p108*
Bemo
Connections with the Bertais terminal in Cakranegara. From Bayan bemos run up to Batu Koq. Bemos also run east from here along the very scenic coastal road to Labuhan Lombok. From the looks of surprise it is clear that few *orang putih* make this (long) journey.

Mount Rinjani *p108*
Bemo
For the more usual north route, take a bemo from the **Bertais** terminal to Bayan, and then a 2nd bemo from Bayan to Senaru. Alternatively, walk from Bayan. For the east route, take a bemo from Labuhan Lombok to Sembalun Bumbung.

Taxi
A taxi from Bangsal to Senaru should cost about US$16.

Kuta Beach and around

Kuta beach, also sometimes known as Putri Nyale beach, is situated among some of the most spectacular coastal scenery on Lombok; rocky outcrops and cliff faces give way to sheltered sandy bays, ideal for swimming and surfing.

Kuta Beach and around → *For listings, see pages 113-115. Phone code: 0370.*

Kuta itself has a stretch of sand on Lombok's south coast, in a bay with a little fishing village at its head. There is a substantial fishing fleet of sailing boats with brightly decorated dugout hulls and outriggers. There are no 'sights' other than the Sasak villages about 20 minutes' drive inland, beside the main Mataram to Kuta road.

The beach is the focal point of a strange annual festival, called the **Bau Nyale**, when thousands of seaworms come to the surface of the sea. Local people flock here to witness the event, and it is becoming quite a popular tourist attraction. See Festivals and events, page 114.

Still a relatively quiet place to stay, there is a good road linking it to Mataram with regular shuttle bus connections.

At present the roads beyond Kuta are poor. The coast road continues east from Kuta past some magnificent, white sandy bays. After 2 km a potholed tarmac road turns off to **Seger Beach**, one of the beaches where the Nyale fish come ashore.

Further on again by 4 km, past low-lying swampy land, is the fine gold-sand beach at **Tanjung Aan**, set in a horseshoe-shaped bay; it is good for swimming, though there are stones and coral about 10 m out. Despite its distance from any development there are

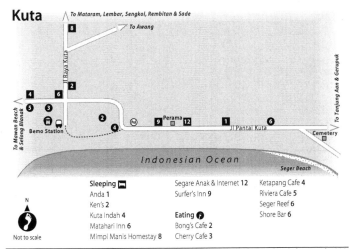

Kuta

To Mataram, Lembar, Sengkol, Rembitan & Sade

To Awang

Jl Raya Kuta

To Mawan Beach & Selong Blanak

To Tanjung Aan & Gerupuk

Bemo Station

Perama

Jl Pantai Kuta

Cemetery

Indonesian Ocean

Seger Beach

N

Not to scale

Sleeping 🛏
Anda **1**
Ken's **2**
Kuta Indah **4**
Matahari Inn **6**
Mimpi Manis Homestay **8**

Segare Anak & Internet **12**
Surfer's Inn **9**

Eating 🍴
Bong's Cafe **2**
Cherry Cafe **3**

Ketapang Cafe **4**
Riviera Cafe **5**
Seger Reef **6**
Shore Bar **6**

stalls, and hawkers materialize as soon as any foreigners appear. **Note** There is no shade on any of these beaches, just basic scrub. The track bends round to the south and ends at **Gerupak (Desert) Point**.

There are many walks in the area: climb the hill immediately to the west of Kuta for spectacular views over the south coast. The **Seger Hills**, 2 km to the east, have numerous farm trails and a small cemetery; near Seger Beach is a rocky promontory with more superb views, especially at sunset.

There are several good surfing beaches. The best are: **Are Guling**, **Mawi**, **Mawun** and **Selong Blanak**. **Gerupak (Desert Point)** is rated as one of the best surf spots in the world outside Hawaii. Kuta was originally 'discovered' by surfers.

Traditional villages that can be visited include: **Sade** and **Rembitan**, 9 km north of Kuta just off the main Mataram road, 20 minutes' drive.

Safety There is an 'honoured' tradition of inter-village theft in these parts. A thief from one village gained prestige by successfully stealing from other villages. Be very careful if out walking after dark. Take extra precautions to safeguard money and valuables. However, all over Lombok local neighbourhood watch-style groups have formed, and will get your stolen goods back within the day. Hence crime has decreased considerably.

West of Kuta

There is now a sealed road running west of Kuta as far as Selong Blanak. Along the way there are several good beaches, all fairly deserted. The occasional bemo runs to Selong Blanak from Praya. Twenty minutes' drive (10 km) west of Kuta is **Mawan Beach**. A perfect horseshoe-shaped bay with a golden sand beach, a large tree and two bamboo shelters (called *garuga*) and several coconut palms offering some protection from the sun. Good for swimming, very protected though the sea bed slopes steeply near the shore. The road west climbs steeply out of Kuta, with spectacular views of the south coast and mist-covered hills in the rainy season. Further west near Selong Blanak are more good gold-sand beaches at **Mawi** and **Rowok**. Mawi in particular offers good surfing. The road continues to the fishing village of **Selong Blanak**, with its wide, sandy bay and accommodation a little inland. Few travellers make the trip further west to **Pengantap**, **Sepi** and **Blongas**; the last of which has good surfing, snorkelling and diving, though be wary of sharks. From Sepi the poor road heads inland via Sekatong to the port of **Lembar**. All roads deteriorate west of Pengantap and should probably be avoided in the wet season. There are some bemos, though most people get here by private or chartered transport. The better accommodation offers free transport to Tanjung Aan Beach to the east and Mawan Beach to the west.

East of Kuta

Shortly before Tanjung Aan the road forks; taking the left fork, northeast, the road passes through Sereneng en route to **Awang**, 18 km from Kuta. The right fork goes to **Gerupak** about 9 km east of Kuta. From here there are boats across Gumbang Bay to **Bumgang** for about US$5.50. From Bumgang there is a path north which connects with the road to Awang. The villagers in this area make their living from fishing and seaweed farming and will hire out boats for about US$25 a day. A few bemos travel these routes and their numbers are slowly increasing, but the best way to see the area is with your own transport.

From Awang, boats can be chartered across the bay to Ekas for about US$12 return. **Ekas** has good surfing and snorkelling. There are spectacular views from the cliffs overlooking Awang Bay on both sides, particularly from Ekas. It is possible but time-consuming to reach

Ekas by public bemo: from Praya, catch a bemo bound for Tanjung Luar and Gubukdalem, get off just before Keruak at the turning south to Jerowaru and wait for a bemo going to Ekas, which is en route to Kaliantan in the southwest corner of the peninsula.

Kuta beach and around listings

For Sleeping and Eating price codes and other relevant information, see pages 7-10.

● Sleeping

Kuta Beach *p111, map p111*
Accommodation options have improved as Kuta's profile as a destination rises. The new airport in central Lombok, set to be completed by the end of 2011, will make Kuta a much easier destination to reach, and should bring in greater investment. Many of the older established hotels here have struggled with maintenance and are slowly becoming faded. However, in recognition of this, their prices have dropped considerably, and it is possible to find some excellent value accommodation. Many of the popular budget surfer hotels are strung out along the beachside road.

$$$ Ken's Hotel, Jln Raya Kuta, T0370 655057. This new hotel caters mainly for Japanese surfers, and the owner is very knowledgeable about the area. The a/c rooms are large and clean, with TV and fridge. The more expensive suites are enormous and have 2 bathrooms. Service here is very efficient, and the kitchen serves up a couple of good Japanese dishes. There is a small but stylish pool and sunbathing area, with showers. Recommended.

$$$-$$ Matahari Inn, Jln Pantai Kuta, T0370 655000. Beautiful gardens, with plenty of lush greenery and Buddha statues reclining and meditating on plinths. Faded rooms, the cheaper ones are musty, dark and charmless. Things improve as you go up the price range. Pool.

$$ Kuta Indah, Jln Pantai Kuta, T0370 653781. This place was built with grand ideas in mind, but lack of custom has forced the owners to slash rates considerably. The a/c and fan rooms are good value, and the pool is extremely inviting.

$$-$ Surfer's Inn, Jln Pantai Kuta, T0370 655582, www.lombok-surfersinn.com. Very popular with a nice pool and lounging area. Rooms are very simple and fairly large. Can arrange surfing lessons.

$ Anda, Jln Pantai Kuta, T0370 654836. Packed with chest-thumping surfers glued to the TV watching waves, this place definitely caters to a niche market, and is obviously succeeding. Rooms are bare and simple.

$ Mimpi Manis Homestay, Desa Mong, T0818 369950, www.mimpimanis.com. It's a shame there aren't more lodgings like this in Indonesia, with extraordinarily friendly staff, good grub, a couple of choice volumes on the bookshelf, and a genuine homestay atmosphere. There are 2 rooms and a house on offer here, all of which are clean and come with TV and DVD player (there is a large library of films to choose from). It's 2 km inland, but the staff will drop you at the beach, and it is a cheap ojek ride back. Excellent value. Highly recommended.

$ Segare Anak, Jln Pantai Kuta, T0370 654846. The cheaper bungalows are wobbling on their stilts, but the slightly more expensive concrete rooms at the back are huge and clean and the bathrooms have a bath. Pool and badminton.

● Eating

Kuta Beach *p111, map p111*
Most places in Kuta have almost identical menus, and the town is certainly no gourmet paradise. Nevertheless, it's easy to fill the belly for less than many places in Lombok, but cast your eyes over the cleanliness of a place before choosing

to eat there. There are an awful lot of flies and rubbish around.

Most of the hotels offer food, although the kitchens usually close earlier than the restaurants. **Ken's Hotel ($$)** whips up a few Japanese dishes, as well as some Indonesian and international favourites; **Mimpi Manis ($)** does a great *nasi campur*.

Be careful of the *warungs* on the beach, some tourists have reported cases of food poisoning after eating in them.

$ Bong's Café, Jln Pantai Kuta, T0819 1611 5552. Open 0800-2300. Friendly place serving wood-fired pizza, sandwiches and lots of good Indonesian fare. Surf films shown.

$ Cherry Café, Jln Pantai Kuta, T0878 6516 8341. Open 0800-2300. Lots of local options and a good salad menu at this friendly Balinese place.

$ Ketapang Café, Jln Pantai Kuta, T0370 655194. Open 0800-2100. This popular restaurant has a seaview and a menu favouring those starved of carbs, with good burgers, pizza and pasta dishes dominating.

$ Riviera Café, Jln Pantai Kuta. Open 0730-2300. A large and diverse menu in a spartan but friendly café near the **Matahari Hotel**. All the usual suspects are on offer here plus a few interesting local dishes such as *ayam taliwang* and *nasi begibung*. Happy hour 1800-2000.

$ Seger Reef, Jln Pantai Kuta, T0370 655528. Open 0800-2200. Lots of Indonesian food and pizza.

$ The Shore Bar, next door to Seger Reef. Open 0800-2400. Good, fresh seafood.

🍸 Bars and clubs

Kuta Beach *p111, map p111*
Nightlife is pretty thin on the ground. **The Shore Bar** (see Eating) is the place to be on Fri nights with live music, lots of surfers and local boys and even the occasional female. **Riviera Café** (see Eating) has live acoustic music on Wed and Fri evenings during the high season. Cultural shows are put on from time to time at the hotels.

✷ Festivals and events

Kuta Beach *p111, map p111*
Feb/Mar (19th day of the 10th month of the Sasak lunar calendar) **Nyale ceremony**, thousands of mysterious sea worms called Nyale fish (*Eunice viridis*) 'hatch' on the reef and rise to the surface of the sea off Kuta. According to the legend of Putri Nyale, the episode is linked to the beautiful Princess Nyale, who drowned herself here after failing to choose between a bevy of eligible men. The worms are supposed to represent her hair, and celebrations are held each year to mark her death. Traditionally, this was a time for young people to find a partner for marriage, and it is still an occasion when the usual strictures controlling contact between the sexes are eased. The worms are scooped from the sea and eaten.

🛍 Shopping

Kuta Beach *p111, map p111*
Local shops along the beachfront sell basics, including fruit, at reasonable prices. An endless stream of young children offer locally woven sarongs of variable quality, T-shirts and fruit. The pineapples here are delicious, as are the green bananas (to tell green bananas from unripe yellow bananas just squeeze; the ripe green bananas will feel soft). Kuta has its market on Sat.

⛰ Activities and tours

Kuta Beach *p111, map p111*
Cycling
There are a couple of bikes for rent at **Mimpi Manis** (see Sleeping) for 25,000Rp per day.

Fishing
Mimpi Manis (see Sleeping) offers the chance to go out with a local fisherman in his *perahu* to catch some fish and take it back to the hotel for a feast. Price is per boat rather than per person, and represents a

good deal compared to fishing trips at many other places on Lombok (whole day US$80).

Fishing
Many people come to Kuta to surf. Boards, lessons, boat travel, repairs and nightly videos of the biggest tubes and breaks in the world are on offer at the **Kimen Surf Shop**, T0370 655064.

⊖ Transport

Kuta Beach *p111, map p111*
Bemo
Public bemo to **Praya** from the bemo stop several times a day, about 8000Rp, 1 hr, from there you can catch a bemo to **Bertais**, 30 mins. Public bemos also connect Kuta with **Labuan Lombok** (for ferries to **Sumbawa**). Most people opt for the shuttle option (below), which is far less hassle.

Bemo services are increasing and more villages are coming on line, especially along the coast roads east and west of Kuta. Best to hire your own transport, though be aware that roads are bumpy. You can hire a car with driver, but self-drive is recommended here; the local drivers have limited skills for the most part. Mataram to Kuta is just over 1 hr, depending on traffic.

Motorbike
Available to hire, often at very reasonable prices, eg 40,000Rp per day. Ask at your accommodation.

Ojek
It's easy to charter an ojek to **Senggigi** or **Mataram** for US$14 (1½ hrs) and stop to see the weaving village of Sukarara on the way. There are usually some fascinating local markets you can stop at along the way back, if you leave early enough. Ask your driver.

Shuttle
Daily **Perama** shuttles to **Mataram** and **Senggigi** leave at 0700 (US$12.50) for connections to **Bali** and the **Gilis**, the **Perama** office is in the Segara Anak Hotel.

Flores and around

Flores stretches over 350 km from east to west, but at most only 70 km from north to south. It is one of the most beautiful islands in the Lesser Sundas. Mountainous, with steep-sided valleys cut through by fast-flowing rivers, dense forests and open savanna landscapes, Flores embraces a wide range of ecological zones. One of the local names for the island is Nusa Nipa or 'Serpent Island', because of its shape.

Ins and outs

Overland transport on Flores, 375 km in length, is neither quick nor comfortable. The Trans-Flores Highway is quite bearable, though travelling on it once is usually enough for most people. The road twists and turns through breathtaking scenery for more than 700 km. The Highway stretches from Labuanbajo in the east to Larantuka in the west.

Labuanbajo → *For listings, see pages 118-121. Phone code: 0385.*

Labuanbajo, or Bajo, is really just an overgrown fishing village. However, it marks the beginning of Eastern Indonesia, with Melanesian features and culture starting to dominate, and Christianity becoming the major religion (often blended with fascinating animist elements), with wonderful tropical churches and friendly nuns in the streets. The views of the harbour and surrounding islands are beautiful, making this one of Indonesia's most alluring harbour towns. There are some reasonable beaches, with excellent offshore snorkelling. It is also an excellent base from which to explore Komodo and Rinca, or to join a boat tour via the reserve and other islands on the way to Lombok. The town is stretched out along one road that runs from the dock, along the seashore, and then south towards Ruteng. **Pramuka Hill**, behind the town, offers good views over the bay, especially at sunset.

Tourist information is available from the **PHKA information booth** ① *on the main street, opposite Gardena Hotel*. It can also provide information on Komodo and Rinca.

Around Labuanbajo

Waicicu Beach lies 15 minutes by boat north of town and offers good snorkelling and diving. One-day trips to the islands **Bidadari** and **Sabobo** can be arranged through hotels or tour operators (on the main road), US$55 per boat for return boat ride. There is good snorkelling in clear waters, and you will potentially have the island to yourself.

Overnight stays on **Seraya Island**, sleeping in bungalows on stilts, can be arranged through **Gardena Hotel** (see Sleeping, page 118).

Komodo → *For listings, see pages 118-121.*

The principal reason people come to Komodo is to see the illustrious Komodo dragon. However, there is more to the reserve than giant lizards and the islands has good trekking, swimming and snorkelling. The park covers 59,000 ha, and is made up not just of Komodo

Island, but also Rinca and a number of other surrounding islets. The highest peak on this rugged spot is Mount Satalibo (735 m).

Ins and outs
It is necessary to charter a boat from Labuanbajo (visit the Komodo Park offices in Labuanbajo for advice), or join a tour to get to the island. The rich and famous arrive direct by helicopter.

Komodo National Park
ⓘ www.komodonationalpark.org. The island is a national park and visitors must register and buy an entrance ticket (US$15 plus US$4.50 valid for 3 days) on arrival at Loh Liang on Komodo, or Loh Buaya on Rinca. The Park HQ at Loh Liang consists of an office, information centre, 4 bungalows, a souvenir shop, church and mosque, and a restaurant.

After the luxuriant vegetation of Bali, Komodo can come as a bit of a shock – at least during the dry season. The islands of the Komodo archipelago are dry and rainfall is highly seasonal. For much of the year, therefore, the grasslands are burnt to dust and interspersed with drought-resistant savannah trees such as the distinctive lontar palm. In contrast the seas are highly productive, so there is good snorkelling, particularly off **Pantai Merah** and **Pulau Lasa**, a small island near Komodo village. The iridescent blue of the water, set against the dull brown of the islands, provides a striking backdrop. However, this image of Komodo as barren is transformed during the short wet season, when rainfall encourages rapid growth and the formerly parched landscape becomes green and lush.

Despite the other attractions of Komodo, it is still the **dragons** that steal the show. They are easily seen, with Timor deer (their chief natural prey) wandering among them. Other wildlife includes land crabs, wild pigs, black drongos, white-bellied sea eagles, and cockatoos, evidence that this is part of the Australasian faunal world. Monkeys are absent.

Walks
The most accessible viewing spot is the dry river bed at **Banu Nggulung**, 30 minutes' walk (2 km) from the accommodation at Loh Liang. Guides can take you there for a small fee, depending on the size of your group (30,000Rp per person). **Note** Visitors are only allowed to walk alone along marked trails. Those wishing to hike off the trails, and see the dragons in a more natural setting, must hire a guide. This is not just to generate income for the wardens; there have been fatalities. For around US$10 per person (but highly negotiable) a guide can take you to **Poreng Valley**, a 7-km walk from the PHKA office. There is a reasonably good chance of spotting a dragon and even if you don't, you will see plenty of other wildlife. There is a short 30-minute walk along the beach from Loh Liang bungalows to the stilt village of **Kampong Komodo**, which can be done without a guide. **Mount Ara** can be climbed in less than two hours (8.5 km to the summit)

Rinca Island → For listings, see pages 118-121.

Ins and outs
Some boats travelling from Lombok to Flores stop off here. Ask about chartering a boat at the **Princess office** ⓘ Jln Kasimo 3, T0385 41744. Rinca Island can also be reached from Komodo.

Wildlife
Rinca Island has a wider range of wildlife than Komodo, including wild horses, water buffaloes and dragons, and has the added advantage of fewer tourists. Only very simple

food is available, so take your own snacks. It is more likely that you will go as part of an organized tour (arranged in Labuanbajo or Lombok) and therefore you will be catered for. Rinca is fast gaining popularity over Komodo and recent visitors have been highly complimentary about trips there.

Flores and around listings

For Sleeping and Eating price codes and other relevant information, see pages 7-10.

🛏 Sleeping

Labuanbajo *p116*
Accommodation in Labuanbajo is generally poor value for money, particularly when compared with Bali and Lombok.
$$$$ Jayakarta Suites, T021 649 0101, www.jayakartahotelresorts.com. Standing somewhat at odds with the overall ambience of the town and its environs is this smart, modern hotel with comfy a/c overlooking the bay. Tennis courts, pools, bar and even a volleyball court to stretch the muscles before heading out to explore
$$ Chez Felix Hotel, T0385 41032. Set in spacious grounds on a hill above the town. The restaurant here has fine views. This is a peaceful place to stay, and all the rooms are tiled, clean and fairly spacious, although they face each other. The beds in the cheaper rooms are a little wobbly.
$$ Golo Hilltop, T0385 41337, www.golo hilltop.com. Located up a dirt track to the north of the town, the views at sunset from here are amazing. The more expensive rooms are comfortable, well decorated and have fan and a/c and Wi-Fi access. Recommended.
$$ Hotel Wisata, Jln Soekarno Hatta, T0385 41020. Indonesian-style hotel, with huge clean rooms, toilets that almost flush and friendly staff. The rooms face each other, so be prepared for some eyeballing.
$$-$ Gardena, Jln Yos Sudarso, T0385 41258. Simple bungalows perched on the hillside overlooking the harbour, have great views but are in dire need of some maintenance. This is the most popular hotel

in town, and is a nice retreat from the dusty main strip. Bathrooms have a mixture of squat and Western toilets (without seats or flush). Tourists have reported things going missing from their verandas and rooms. The hotel has a safety box. Often full.
$ Bajo Beach Hotel, T0385 41008. This hotel takes the overspill from the **Gardena**. It's a rambling place with friendly, if somewhat eccentric staff. The simple tiled rooms have mosquito net, and bathroom with toilet (no flush), *mandi* and shower. Also rents snorkel equipment.

Seraya Island
$$-$ Seraya Island Bungalows, T0385 41258, www.serayaisland.com. 12 very simple bungalows on a lovely beach with superb snorkelling nearby. Many visitors struggle to leave this place. There is a 2-night minimum stay, and transport there and back costs 50,000Rp. Contact the **Gardena** to book.

Sape
Sape is used as an overnight stop by travellers that have taken a leisurely trip across Sumbawa, and missed the early morning ferry connection to Flores (see page 120).
$ Losmen Mutiara, right by the port entrance, T0374 71337. Clean simple rooms, more expensive with a/c. There are few places to eat nearby.

Komodo *p116*
It is very rare for people to stay the night on Komodo nowadays. If you wish to do so, contact the PHKA office in Labuanbajo beforehand. The only accommodation on Komodo is in the **PHKA bungalows ($)** at

Loh Liang, which has a capacity of about 40. They are simple but clean bungalows in a beautiful bay. Electricity from 1800 to 2200. Bedding consists of mattresses on the floor. During the peak season Jul-Sep, visitors must sleep in the dining room. Some rooms have their own *mandi* for no extra cost. The quality of the rooms is not great, but if you have the time, it is worth staying on the island. The cafeteria provides basic and rather overpriced food.

Camping There is also a campground at Loh Liang.

Rinca Island *p117*

Most people visit Rinca on a day-trip rather than staying the night.
$ PHKA bungalows, Loh Buaya. Basic accommodation, these stilted wooden cabins are the haunts of various rodent and insect populations, so be prepared.

Eating

Labuanbajo *p116*

Most of the hotels have a restaurant, but quality varies enormously. There is a huge number of *nasi Padang* places in Labuanbajo. Poke your head behind the lace curtain to check the freshness first.
$$ The Lounge, T0385 41962. Open 0800-2300. With a breezy harbour view, this relaxing place has a limited menu of Western food featuring fair burritos, feta salad and home-made ciabatta bread. Films are shown here occasionally and the staff are very friendly and keen to practise their English.
$ Gardena, Jln Yos Sudarso, T0385 41258. Open 0730-2200. The most popular travellers' hangout in town, with great views, enormous fish hot plates and cheap salads. This is a very social spot, and a great place to meet other people in order to form a group for a trip to Komodo, or the island's interior. Recommended.
$ Matahari, T0385 41008. Open 0800-2200. Cheap pasta, seafood and soup with a wonderful view of the harbour.

Bars and clubs

Labuanbajo *p116*

Paradise Bar, T0385 41533. Open 24 hrs. Up a dirt track on the north side of the town, on the way to the **Golo Hilltop**, this is the place for connoisseurs of fine sunsets and cold beer. The views are truly beautiful. Sat night is when the bar comes alive, as locals and tourists head here in droves to listen to live acoustic and reggae music.

Shopping

Labuanbajo *p116*

Between 0630 and 0900, multiple stalls set up along the main road selling vegetables. The usual shops can be found. There is a small choice of sarongs and woven cloth; and a good shop for wooden carvings, including some rather gruesome masks. Hawkers linger at the entrance to the **Gardena**, with strings of pearls, and dragon carvings.

Activities and tours

Labuanbajo *p116*
Tour operators

There are a few tour operators offering boat trips as well as inland tours. Labuanbajo is the jumping-off point for journeys into the interior and there are companies offering breakneck 3-day tours of Flores. However, Flores is an island rich in natural beauty and cultural heritage and deserves more time to be spent on it. It is easy enough to organize independent travel around the island.
Lestari Jaya, at entrance to **Gardena Hotel**, T0852 3900 5498. Offers 4-day/3-night boat tours to Bangsal (Lombok), stopping at Komodo, Rinca and Pulau Moyo and Pulau Satonda (Sumbawa) en route, around US$150 per person. Food is included, but admission fee to the Komodo National Park isn't. Check out the boat before agreeing to a tour; some boats are overloaded. It also has a trip that takes in

Bajawa, Moni and Kelimutu for US$260 (per group, 4 people maximum). **Perama**, T0385 42016. Runs a 2-day trip to Lombok via Rinca costing US$130 for a spot on the deck and US$180 for a cabin. They also offer 4-day tours into the interior of the beautiful island of Flores calling in at Ruteng, Ende, Moni, Kelimutu and finally Maumere for US$360 per car (maximum 4 people). For those who just wish to cruise around Komodo **Perama** offers a 2-night/ 3-day trip costing US$250 per person. **Princess**, Jln Kasimo 3, T0385 41744. Has a boat for charter to Komodo and Rinca. Snorkelling equipment provided.

Komodo *p116*
Diving and snorkelling

The waters around Komodo are finally getting the recognition they deserve as having some of the finest diving spots in the world. The local diving industry is growing by the year with more and more foreign investors opening up businesses. The waters around the national park are teeming with life and, with improved accessibility over recent years, are seeing increasing numbers of visitors, including liveaboards from as far away as Thailand. The reef is considered to be 99% pristine, with strong currents keeping the water temperature down and preventing the blanching effects of El Niño as seen around the Gili islands. Most companies operate day trips back and forth from Labuanbajo (see Boat, opposite), rather than operating as liveaboards, although this option is available. It takes 1½-2 hrs to reach sites around Komodo. Typically a day trip with 2 dives costs around US$80. Packages are available for 3, 5, and 10 days. Highly recommended are **Reefseekers**, T0385 41433, www.reefseekers.net, whose British owners enthuse about marine life and offer 1½-hr briefings on the journey to the reef on the ecology of the reef relevant to the area being visited. They have built a top notch resort on Pulau Bidadari, which has

brought the diving even closer. Also recommended are **Bajo Dive Club**, T0385 41503, www.komododiver. com, and **Dive Komodo**, T0385 41862, www.divekomodo.com.

Note Divers should be warned that currents around the Komodo National Park can be very strong and may not be suitable for inexperienced divers. In Jun 2008, 5 European divers were swept away from their boat in a rip tide. After 9 hrs adrift they managed to get to a remote beach on Rinca where they fought off Komodo dragons and survived on a diet of shellfish for 2 days before being rescued.

There is some great snorkelling off the nearby islands, and around Pantai Merah and Pulau Bidadari in the national park. You need to charter a boat to do this, which can cost between US$50 to US$80. Enquire at one of the agents around town.

⊖ Transport

Labuanbajo *p116*
Air

Komodo Airport is 2 km from town. Airport departure tax is 10000Rp. Flights are met by minivans, and private vehicles. It costs around 15,000Rp to get to the airport from the town. Between **Merpati**, on the way to the airport, T0385 41177; **Indonesia Air Transport**, Jln Kasimo, T0385 41088; and **Trans Nusa**, Jln Soekarno Hatta, T0385 41800, there are daily connections to **Denpasar**. If you want to head to Lombok or Java you must transit in Bali. **Wings Air** (book online through **Lion Air** at www. lionair.co.id) also offers daily connections with Denpasar. **Merpati** is notorious for cancellations. Flights get booked out in advance, so booking early is essential.

Boat

Daily ferries leave at 0800 for **Sape**, **Sumbawa**, 6-8 hrs, US$4-7 depending on class. Buses meet the ferry from Sape and take passengers straight on to Ruteng. Boats travel frequently between Labuanbajo and Lombok, via Komodo on tours. The PELNI vessel *Tilongkabila* docks at Labuanbajo twice a month travelling alternately westwards to **Bima**, **Lembar** and **Benoa** (Bali) and northwards to **Sulawesi** with a handy connection to **Makassr**. The PELNI office, T0385 41106, is up a small dirt track past the football pitch. It is in a mechanic's workshop and not signposted.

Bus
There is no bus station; buses cruise the hotels and *losmen* picking up passengers. There are connections with **Ruteng**, 4 hrs, and **Bajawa**, 10 hrs, 1 daily at 0600 – book at any of the tourist information offices in town. It is even possible to make the exhausting journey all the way to **Ende** on a bus that meets the ferry from Sape.

Lansung Indah, T0385 41106, has a small outlet in a mobile phone shop near the port entrance. It sells bus/ferry combination tickets for **Bima**, **Mataram**, **Denpasar**, **Surabaya** and even **Jakarta**.

To Flores from Lombok via Sape, (**Sumbawa**) Many tourists opt to take an overnight bus from Lombok and across Sumbawa on the way to Flores. Typically, buses depart from Mataram (Lombok) around 1500 and travel across Lombok and Sumbawa (with a 2-hr ferry crossing between) arriving in Bima around 0400. Most travellers book a through ticket (Mataram–Sape), and upon arrival in Bima are put on a small bus for the 2-hr ride to Sape. The Mataram–Sape bus ticket will

need to be shown to the conductor on this minibus, so don't throw the ticket away. The bus should arrive in time for the 0800 ferry to Labuanbajo (Flores). Some tourists find this heavy going and prefer to stay the night in Sape, or, if the bus breaks or is late, have to stay there.

Car hire
Lestari Jaya, (see Activities and tours), and **Manumadi**, Jln Soekarno Hatta, T0385 41457, manumadi@telkom.net, both have vehicles for hire to explore the surrounding countryside.

Ojek
Ojeks for travel around town cost 4000Rp during the day and 7000Rp after sunset.

ⓘ Directory

Labuanbajo *p116*
Banks BNI, main road (150 m towards Ruteng from Bajo Beach Hotel), will change cash and TCs from major companies and has an ATM that accepts foreign cards. It is best to also bring some cash in case this breaks down, as the next ATM is a long way from here. **Internet** Pagi Swalayan, Jln Soekarno Hatta, above the Pagi Swalayan supermarket on the 3rd floor, 0800-2200, this place is roasting but has a reasonable connection at 10,000Rp per hr. **Post office** In the centre of town. **Telephone** Telkom office, south of town, near the PHKA office. Several **Wartel** offices around town.

Contents

124 Index

Footnotes

Index

A
Agung Gianyar Palace 57
Amed 72
Amlapura 76
avian flu 15

B
Bahasa Indonesia 16
Bali, East 79
Bali Aga 60
Balina Beach 74
Balinese pura 66
Bangli 57
Bangsal 93
Baru, Mount 109
Batubelig 28, 35
Batur, Lake 59
Bayan 108
Berewa beach 30
Besakih 65
bilharzia 15
Blanco, Antonio 46
Bukit Jati 59

C
Candi Dasa 74
Canggu 28

D
dengue fever 15
Denpasar 22
diarrhoea 15
diving, Gilis 106
dolphins, Lovina Beach 77

E
East Bali 70

F
Flores 116

G
geringsing 76
Gianyar 57
Gili Air 100
Gili Meno 100
Gili Islands, the 97
    listings 101
Gili Trawangan 99
Goa Lawah 72, 76
Goa Susu 109
Gunung Agung 65, 68
Gunung Ara 117
Gunung Batur 59

H
health 15
    vaccinations 16

I
ikat
    geringsing 76

K
Kamasan village 72
Kambing, Nusa (goat
    island) 76
Karangasem 70
Kartini Day 12
Kedisan 60
Kintamani 61, 63
Komodo 116
komodo dragon 117
Kusamba 72
Kuta (Bali) 26
Kuta beach (Lombok) 111

L
Labuanbajo 116
Legian 28
Lembar 112
Lembongan, Nusa 72
Lovina 76

M
malaria 15
Manggis 74
Manggis beach 74
Mawan Beach 112
Moon of Pejeng 50
Mount Rinjani 108

P
Padangbai 73
Pantai, Cecil 73
Pejeng 49
Penelokan 61, 62
Penida, Nusa 72
Petitenget 28
Pura
    Dalem Agung
        Padangtegal 48
Pura Batur 61
Pura Besakih 65
Pura Dalem 59
Pura Gunung Kawi 62
Purajati 59
Pura Kehen 58
Pura Saraswati 48
Pura Tegeh Koripan 61
Puri Saren 48
Puri Semarapura 71
Putung 74

R
rabies 15
Rinca Island 117
Rinjani, Mount 108
rupiah 17

S
Sacred Monkey Forest
    Sanctuary 48
Sakenan, Pura 32
Sanur 30
SARS 15

schistosomiasis 15
seaweed 101
Sebatu 62
Selong Blanak 112
Semarapura 71
Seminyak 28
Senggigi 92
Sengkidu village 76
Serangan Island 32
Sidan 59
Siri beach 108

sleeping prices 8
surfing
    Canggu 28

T
Tenganan 75
Tirta Empul 50
Tirtagangga 72
Toya Bungkah 59
Trunyan 60
tuberculosis 15

U
Ubud 46

V
vaccinations 16

W
West coast Lombok 92
    listings 94

Titles available in the Footprint *Focus* range

Latin America	UK RRP	US RRP
Bahia & Salvador	£7.99	$11.95
Buenos Aires & Pampas	£7.99	$11.95
Costa Rica	£8.99	$12.95
Cuzco, La Paz & Lake Titicaca	£8.99	$12.95
El Salvador	£5.99	$8.95
Guadalajara & Pacific Coast	£6.99	$9.95
Guatemala	£8.99	$12.95
Guyana, Guyane & Suriname	£5.99	$8.95
Havana	£6.99	$9.95
Honduras	£7.99	$11.95
Nicaragua	£7.99	$11.95
Paraguay	£5.99	$8.95
Quito & Galápagos Islands	£7.99	$11.95
Recife & Northeast Brazil	£7.99	$11.95
Rio de Janeiro	£8.99	$12.95
São Paulo	£5.99	$8.95
Uruguay	£6.99	$9.95
Venezuela	£8.99	$12.95
Yucatán Peninsula	£6.99	$9.95

Asia	UK RRP	US RRP
Angkor Wat	£5.99	$8.95
Bali & Lombok	£8.99	$12.95
Chennai & Tamil Nadu	£8.99	$12.95
Chiang Mai & Northern Thailand	£7.99	$11.95
Goa	£6.99	$9.95
Hanoi & Northern Vietnam	£8.99	$12.95
Ho Chi Minh City & Mekong Delta	£7.99	$11.95
Java	£7.99	$11.95
Kerala	£7.99	$11.95
Kolkata & West Bengal	£5.99	$8.95
Mumbai & Gujarat	£8.99	$12.95

Africa & Middle East	UK RRP	US RRP
Beirut	£6.99	$9.95
Damascus	£5.99	$8.95
Durban & KwaZulu Natal	£8.99	$12.95
Fès & Northern Morocco	£8.99	$12
Jerusalem	£8.99	$12
Johannesburg & Kruger National Park	£7.99	$11
Kenya's beaches	£8.99	$12
Kilimanjaro & Northern Tanzania	£8.99	$12
Zanzibar & Pemba	£7.99	$11

Europe	UK RRP	US
Bilbao & Basque Region	£6.99	$9.
Granada & Sierra Nevada	£6.99	$9.
Málaga	£5.99	$8.95
Orkney & Shetland Islands	£5.99	$8.95
Skye & Outer Hebrides	£6.99	$9.95

North America	UK RRP	US RRP
Vancouver & Rockies	£8.99	$12.95

Australasia	UK RRP	US RRP
Brisbane & Queensland	£8.99	$12.95
Perth	£7.99	$11.95

For the latest books, e-books and smart phone app releases, and a wealth of travel information, visit us at:
www.footprinttravelguides.com.

footprinttravelguides.com

Join us on facebook for the latest travel news, product releases, offers and amazing competitions: www.facebook.com/footprintbooks.com.